Between a Man and a Woman

&

F*ckingLifeMate

The Plays of Scott James

The Bread & Roses Theatre
68 Clapham Manor Street
London SW4 6DZ
www.breadandrosestheatre.co.uk

Between a Man and a Woman & **F*ckingLifeMate**. *The Plays of Scott James.*

© Scott James.

First published by The Bread & Roses Theatre in 2018.

Scott James has asserted his right to be identified as the author of this work. All rights reserved. Requests to re produce the text in whole or in part should be addressed to the publisher.

Cover photography by: Robert Piwko Photography
Cover model: Kelsey Short
Design/Formatting: Tessa Hart

ISBN 978-1-912504-00-8

Amateur and Professional Performing Rights

No performance of any kind of either play may be given unless a licence has been obtained, including excerpts and readings. Application should be made before rehearsals begin. Publication of these plays does not indicate availability for performance. This applies to all mediums and all languages.

To enquire about availability for performing rights and the necessary steps to undertake to obtain a licence, please contact info@breadandrosestheatre.co.uk in the first instance.

Scott James

Scott James trained as an actor at Trinity Laban Conservatoire of Music and Dance.

"Between a Man and a Woman" was his first full length play. He has previously written for the original workshop of 'Spectrum' (Scartlet Productions) and written for student and short films.

Also a theatre director, he has directed productions of 'Little Shop of Horrors', 'RENT' and 'Rabbit Hole' as well as running his own company, JamesArts Productions.

Between a Man and a Woman & *F*ckingLifeMate*. *The Plays of Scott James.*

Between a Man and a Woman

A play by Scott James

Between a Man and a Woman & F*ckingLifeMate. The Plays of Scott James.

BETWEEN A MAN AND A WOMAN was originally presented by JamesArts Productions as a workshop at the Battersea Barge, London (UK), from 25th to 27th September 2016.

The first fully staged production run took place at the Bread & Roses Theatre, London (UK), from 4th to 14th January 2017 (official opening 6th January 2017) with a performance at the Etcetera Theatre on 16th January 2017.

It was presented with the following cast and creatives:

Creatives
Written and Directed by
Scott James

Choreographed by
Cristian Valle

Produced by
John McLaren & Scott James

Stage Management/Tech
Hannah Wallis & Eoghan Lawlor

Cast
TOM
Millin Thomas

POLLY
Emily Rose Pankhurst

HARRY
Sam Stay

TAMMY
Julie Cloke

CHRIS
Matthew Stewart

SIOBHAN
Laura Janes

SHELLY
Samantha Jacobs

ANNA
Sophia Handscomb

JOSH
Lewis Lilley

NATALIE/LINDA/CATHY
Scarlett Maltman

Understudies: Scarlett Maltman/Scott James/Samantha Jacobs

Special Thanks also to Emilie Nutley, Kelsey Short, Nathan Lister, Charlotte E Tayler, Samantha Jacobs, Roisin Gardner, Euan Bennet, Jasmin Gleeson, Greg Arudnell, Rosie Spivey.

<u>**Between a Man and a Woman & F*ckingLifeMate. The Plays of Scott James.**</u>

Characters

TOM

POLLY

HARRY

TAMMY

CHRIS

SIOBHAN

SHELLY

ANNA

JOSH

NATALIE

LINDA

CATHY

Between a Man and a Woman & F*ckingLifeMate. The Plays of Scott James.

The ensemble stand lifeless. The company begin to weave in and out of each other, surrounding TOM & POLLY. The company perform various repeated movements to signify lust, anger, attack and sadness. Everyone stops. They stand lifeless.

TOM
I know you probably won't respond to this message.

HARRY
The thing with my brother is that he's always needed this. I've never seen him smile so much.

SIOBHAN
Please pick up the phone. I need to know where I stand. I need to know what's going on here.

TAMMY
He has a hold over her that no-one has ever had. Something about her behaviour recently just worries me; surely you must see it too?

The following lines are said within close proximity of each other. Lines are delivered to POLLY & TOM.

HARRY
Tom, you've got it. You've finally escaped/ and now you can move on. That's all behind us now. The hold over us is gone, we can be happy.

TAMMY
Polly, I need you to understand that I am looking out for you - I want you to be safe/ and I don't feel that you are safe at the moment. Please Polly. Come outside and talk to me.

SIOBHAN
This is ridiculous- you need to decide what you want/, because I don't know if you're even sure yourself.

A spotlight beams onto TOM.

TOM
I married you and I was the happiest I had ever been. There were demons that had haunted me - controlled my life and made my very existence a misery, but when I was with you - I barely even thought of them. You made me a new man - and you know what, suddenly I liked what I saw in the mirror.

Between a Man and a Woman & *F*ckingLifeMate*. *The Plays of Scott James.*

The COMPANY begin to move.

POLLY
The moment you took me to that cute little restaurant down some little country lane in Sevenoaks, I knew I wanted to spend the rest of my life with you - you looked into my eyes and I saw a beautiful person that I had the hugest love for. I remember the first time you held me; I thought I could stay there forever. So strong, safe, sure. Sweet, so sweet - everything you did you did because you cared.

The lights change and POLLY holds TOM's hand. We get the impression that they are in a doctor's waiting room.

TOM
Hi - we'd like to book an appointment with the nurse practitioner please.

POLLY
Nurse Baker please.

TOM
Yeah, but does she specialise in family planning?

POLLY
I'm sure they can all give the same advice Tom.

TOM
If you're sure?

POLLY
She'll be fine.

They leave the waiting room. TOM holds POLLY.

TOM
We're gonna do it this time.

POLLY
I can't wait.

He kisses her.

Are you sure we're ready?

TOM
It makes perfect sense.

The lighting changes. TOM freezes. The COMPANY begin to circle POLLY, performing their repeated movements. They get faster and faster and eventually slow down and pick up POLLY. They put her down and begin to rewind. TAMMY is lit to indicate a flashback.

TAMMY
Sorry Polly; for my own piece of mind, I've gotta ask you; what happened to your eye?

POLLY
What?

TAMMY
What happened to your eye Pol? You've got a black eye.

POLLY
Oh yeah that. I'm so stupid Tammy. I dropped my flannel as I was getting out the shower, bent down to pick it up and then got up and walked into the shower door. Hurt like hell- I didn't think it would leave a mark though.

TAMMY
Oh. That was silly.

POLLY
Yeah. You know me- you know what I'm like.

TAMMY
How's Tom?

POLLY
Yeah, yeah he's good.
The lights change and we are back to the previous scene.

TOM
We better start thinking of names soon.

POLLY
First things first eh?

The females of the ensemble perform their repeated movements from the beginning and hand POLLY a packet of contraception. The lighting cross fades to TAMMY & CHRIS.

TAMMY
I don't want to.

CHRIS
Yes you do.

TAMMY
No Chris. The last time I spoke to her, she said some really hurtful things to me. It was really awful.

CHRIS
Well, I think it's probably quite safe to say that some of the things you said to her weren't very pleasant.

TAMMY
I was looking out for her. I was telling her what she needed to hear.

CHRIS
Either way - that didn't work out did it?

TAMMY
I'm fully aware of that thank you.

CHRIS
Come on, come and sit down.

TAMMY
All I was saying is that -

CHRIS
Come on Tammy, come and sit down.

TAMMY joins CHRIS on the sofa.

I know what you were saying. You miss her, that's natural. She's your sister and -

TAMMY
But that doesn't mean I am ready to just accept him.

CHRIS
I know that.

TAMMY
I used to go round there and she'd have black eyes and busted lips - how many doors can you walk into? How many times can you fall over in the shower?

CHRIS
We never actually proved that it was him doing that to her.

TAMMY
No, we didn't, you're right. Because he whisked her out of any contact with us before we could get any information out of her.

CHRIS
Well, we know he was stressed at work, and then -

TAMMY
And that logically explains her one day phoning me up and saying that she feels as if her and Tom need space from the two of us as we are suffocating them.

CHRIS
All I am saying is that you- we didn't handle that conversation very well.

TAMMY
No, you feel I didn't handle it well.

CHRIS
Well Tammy, going round to their house and shouting outside for Polly, claiming her husband is a wife-beater probably wasn't the best thing to do.

TAMMY
He didn't even let her come out and talk to me. He answered for her. All the signs add up for me Chris.

CHRIS
Someone needs to extend the olive branch. It won't be them.

They sit in silence.

TAMMY
Fine, I'll ring her.

CHRIS
It doesn't need to be anything big. Maybe invite them to the party on Saturday. Then they won't feel under pressure or as if they're being assessed.

TAMMY
I wish you didn't bring out your head of social care manner at home Chris.

CHRIS
I'm right though aren't I?

Another silence.

TAMMY
Ok. Right. Well here we go then. It's gone straight to voicemail.

CHRIS
Perfect, leave a voicemail then.

TAMMY
But I -

CHRIS
Then she can listen to it, let it sink in.

TAMMY
Fine, I - yeah, hi Polly it's Tammy-

The lights crossfade to POLLY. It is very late. TAMMY stands behind POLLY.

TAMMY
I ummm, I was thinking. Shall we sort this out? Please ring me or text me or just answer me. Please Polly. You're my sister. It's not just my fault. You know that, and then thing is, I can't just...look, you need to understand...I just...we need to sort this. Bye.

POLLY is affected by this. She slowly goes to grab TAMMY's hand, however this is broken at the last minute by TOM calling.

TOM
Polly are you alright? Come back to bed.

She jumps and disregards TAMMY.

The lights change. People rush across the stage, creating an atmosphere of a busy city. Eventually SIOBHAN & TOM are passionately kissing, his trousers are unzipped and her shirt is unbuttoned. POLLY & TAMMY stand awkwardly.

POLLY
Do you want a cup of tea?

TAMMY
That'd be nice thank you.

POLLY
I wish you'd have told me you were coming over. I'd have picked up the house.

TAMMY
That would have been difficult. You been body building then? Sorry, just being facetious.

POLLY
Tammy, I -

TAMMY
Did you get a new number?

POLLY
No, I -

TAMMY
Only, I left you a voicemail.
POLLY
I know.

TAMMY
Why didn't you answer it?

POLLY
I didn't know what to say, if I'm being honest.

TAMMY
It wasn't just my fault Polly.

POLLY
How's Andrew?

TAMMY
He's well. Getting big now.

POLLY
I can imagine. And Chris?

TAMMY
She's good. She'd like to see you.

POLLY
I'll get that tea made.

POLLY stands up and exits to make the tea. As TAMMY watches her leave, one of the female ensemble hand a packet to her.

SIOBHAN & TOM are passionately kissing.

SIOBHAN
Tom- stop for a minute.

TOM
What? But we've not got much-

SIOBHAN
I know, but just - wait one minute.

TOM
What is it?

SIOBHAN
I'm sick of it being like this.

TOM
Like what?

SIOBHAN
You know, this meeting when you've got a spare ten minutes or getting to see you occasionally for a meal.

TOM
You know, I'm just, just busy aren't I?

SIOBHAN
Tom - are you bored of me?

TOM
What are you talking about?

SIOBHAN
It feels like you're losing interest. Or do you just want something casual?

TOM
No, it's not that, it's just that - well it's early days yet.

SIOBHAN
Five months Tom. I want this to go somewhere.

TOM
Look, it's just that -

SIOBHAN
You're seeing someone else aren't you?

The focus switches to POLLY & TAMMY. POLLY re-enters.

TAMMY
Polly; what are these?

POLLY
What are you doing with those?

TAMMY
I'm going to see them if you just leave them about aren't I?

POLLY
You had no right to -

TAMMY
These are Sert-ra-line, yes?

POLLY
Sertraline, yes.

TAMMY
They're anti-depressants.

POLLY
Yes.

TAMMY
So you're unhappy?

POLLY
It doesn't work like that.

TAMMY
Well, what IS making you unhappy?

POLLY
It's not as simple as that.

TAMMY
I could hazard a guess.

POLLY
Oh, here we go.

TAMMY
Well Polly, there is a glaring issue here that you never seem to address.

POLLY
Let me guess - my husband.

TAMMY
Well, you said it, not me. It makes me so worried Polly; I know what happened the last time I tried to-

POLLY
Because you don't understand what Tom and I have. You don't know Tom, not properly.

TAMMY
No, you're right, I don't. I thought I did; he used to worship the ground you walked on. He was devoted. He was wonderful.

POLLY
He still is. Nothing has changed since we got married.

Between a Man and a Woman & F*ckingLifeMate. The Plays of Scott James.

TAMMY
He's broken you away from your friends, your family. Your sister.

POLLY
No Tammy - you've done that yourself. You can't blame Tom for the way you've behaved.

The focus shifts back to SIOBHAN & TOM.

TOM
You're being silly Shiv. Committing is just a big step for me.

SIOBHAN
Ok, yeah, I get that. But like you've never come to mine? I've never been to yours, we've only spent the night together a handful of times. I want to be with you- but this hot and cold, sometimes here and there thing is making me anxious.

TOM
The thing is, we're in completely different parts of London. It's much more convenient for us to stay in central. I can afford it, so why not? It's easier for both of us isn't it?

SIOBHAN
Yeah, but a Premier Inn isn't the same as being in each other's spaces. I always feel like a guest somewhere when I see you, and I shouldn't feel that.

TOM
I do care about you and I know what you mean, I just-

SIOBHAN
I tell you what- just meet my mum and dad. My sister; meet my sister. That's all I ask.

TOM
That's ALL you ask?

SIOBHAN
It's not asking much. Tom, they don't bite. They'll love you. Please, just do this for me.

We switch to POLLY & TAMMY.

TAMMY
And the writing? Hundreds of plastic wallets full of <u>your</u> writing, notebooks full of your work? And where are all of the books? You used to love reading.

POLLY
I was a kid- that's an old dream that never worked out. Nothing to do with Tom; I wasn't good enough. We're gonna start a family. How will I have time to write?

The light changes.

TOM
Is that it? You care more about your books than me?

POLLY
No. No you know that's not true.

TOM
This, this 'career' you talk about. Is it really worth it?

POLLY
Of course it is - it's part of me.

TOM
The heartache? All that rejection you'll get Polly. There are so many people out there who are more dedicated, have the time to do it. I don't want to hurt you Polly, but, look...are you good enough? There's so much competition. I don't want to see you throw this marriage, our marriage away over a career that probably won't happen. Do you want us to work? Do you want us to have a family?

POLLY
I want our marriage to work, of course I do. I want to be a mother- you know I do.

TOM
Then get rid of them. Kids need a mother, a strong force to drive their family. How can you do that if you're writing?

POLLY
Please Tom.

TOM
Well?

Focus changes back to the present.

TAMMY
Who told you that you weren't good enough? Him?

Between a Man and a Woman & *F*ckingLifeMate*. *The Plays of Scott James.*

POLLY
No Tammy - I know I wasn't good enough. I'm going to be a mother. I'm not good enough. I was never that good. There's so much rejection and I couldn't have handled it.

TAMMY
All I can hear is him Polly. This is not Polly talking, it's Tom. You never even wanted children. You've been brainwashed.

POLLY
No. It's not Tom. The only thing he was ever worried about was me being happy, and he knows I wouldn't be happy with rejection. And things change - now I want a baby.

TAMMY
Writing is part of you.

POLLY
Was part of me.

TAMMY
Just make the break Polly. We'll support you. I miss you and when I say I miss you- I mean I miss YOU. The real you; the girl I watched grow up. My sister.

POLLY
I can't believe you - you've actually come into my home to tell me to leave my husband. This is why we don't talk Tammy. Ever since I married Tom you have looked for ways to put him down and belittle him and come between us. Well Tom is right - we don't need this hurt or heartache. Either of us, because you know what Tammy, Tom has always been a perfect gentleman to you. He has never been rude, aggressive or violent towards you. I have no idea where you get these ridiculous ideas from about him.

TAMMY
So, the depression? We just pretend you're not depressed do we?

POLLY
Have you considered that maybe I'm depressed is because my sister just won't accept my choices and my life and then estranges herself from me and my husband. Maybe I'm depressed because you are throwing back everything that my husband did for us - me and you, when our parents died, back in his face.

TAMMY
Polly, I cannot believe you would use that against me- that is how much he has manipulated you; you are now using our dead parents as a weapon. They would be so ashamed of you.

A stunned silence.

TOM
No. Sorry Siobhan. I'm not doing it.

SIOBHAN
This is absurd. We've never been in a completely private location together. Don't. Don't tell me that the hotels are private. Yes, maybe we aren't with other people, but it's still in a neutral location. Neither of our homes. Now as much as I've loved the hotels and I say loved because even properly spending time together is now a thing of the past, it's just got seedier and dirtier because these days I just come here for a quickie. I have loved being treated like a princess, but it doesn't feel real - because you haven't let me in.

TOM
Look if this is about coming here, then yeah, maybe I've been unfair. I'll book us a weekend away and then-

SIOBHAN
Tom, what the fuck? Have you listened to a word I just said? I do not want another hotel. I want to know what the bloody hell is going on in your head. I have had it up to here. You drain me; you make me feel used and dirty, but still, I can't stop thinking about you. Stop messing with my head. Be a man and be honest with me and tell me what the hell is going on.

TOM
I've had enough of this; maybe if you think rationally and stop having a temper tantrum then we can talk about this.

SIOBHAN
You're ridiculous. What a pathetic man you are. "Oh look at me I've got a well-paying job with lots of perks." Did you have a bet with your mates that you could pull a girl who was at uni or something? Lead her on and get her tell you she wanted to get serious. Well you are unbelievable. Pathetic, patronising, stupid, egotistical -

TOM initially laughs this outburst off, but the more personal and spiteful she gets the more he loses his cool. Eventually he loses his temper, stands up walks over to her and fronts her up. SIOBHAN doesn't flinch. She fronts him back.

SIOBHAN
You don't scare me Tom.

TOM
Get out you stupid little girl.

SIOBHAN
With complete pleasure.

She leaves confidently.

POLLY
Get out.

TAMMY
You know what Polly. I told Chris this wouldn't work, but he insisted, because unlike your manipulative and unhinged husband, he wants this family together. That's the difference between your marriage and mine. My wife protects and cares about me. I'm not a prisoner.

POLLY
I want you to leave Tammy.

TAMMY
Why? Got to make the lord and master his dinner? You know what - I'm sick of this. From today; I have no sister. I am done with worrying and crying and, and - you know what, just forget it. It was nice to have a sister once upon a time, but I'm not putting myself through this anymore.

POLLY is shaking. She looks at TOM who addresses TAMMY.

TOM
You need to get out of here Tammy. We don't need your poisonous accusations and spiteful meddling in our life. Your type of relationships must be very different from our types of relationships - you'd never understand. I think you need to take a good look at yourself before you come pointing the finger at us.

TAMMY looks to POLLY. She walks towards her. The lights change.

ANNA
You're really distant today Pol.

POLLY
She hates him. Anna she hates him. She can't accept me being with him. I can't turn my back on my husband, even if she wants me to.

ANNA
Your sister cares about you.

POLLY
We have plans. Like, we've really started planning Anna. We're gonna come off the pill. We're ready for it.

ANNA
Polly this is me you're talking to. Are you sure you're ready?

POLLY
Anna - yeah, yeah we are...no.

ANNA
I helped you pick up the pieces, literally pick up the pieces; when he blew up before.

POLLY
He felt lonely, like I wasn't supporting him and I wasn't. I was writing far too much and I neglected him and our marriage.

ANNA
He ripped up your books.

POLLY
He's settled. He's calm. He's desperate to be a father.

ANNA
He ripped up your work.

The lights change. TOM stands with a piece of paper.

TOM
Let's see what's more important Polly. Our marriage or your mediocre writing. If you value me <u>and</u> our relationship; me doing this shouldn't matter. In fact, it's a blessing.

He rips up the paper.

POLLY
I know to you it may not make sense. But he's ready. It is different.

ANNA studies POLLY. She finally exhales.

ANNA
How's the counselling going?

POLLY
Yeah, it's - it's fine. I just, I find her a bit...yeah - it's fine.

ANNA
You told Tom yet?

POLLY is silent.

Look, Tom could surprise you - us, he could surprise all of us. Maybe...look, the doctor said grief counselling can help, I don't know -

POLLY
It's been two years Anna. It would break his hurt. He'd feel like it was him.

ANNA
But maybe it -

POLLY
Jeez, I better go.

ANNA
Whatever you say Polly. I will support you whatever. I just want you to be happy. Come over and see Mel soon. She misses you.

A spotlight beams on HARRY.

HARRY
You know what? All these years I've held my tongue; I've held in what I really feel. You've really had a hold over everyone my whole life haven't you? Well look at you - you're ridiculous. You are just ridiculous. I've grown up wanting, no fucking NEEDING a reason to be happy. That's something you just can't offer. Does it feel good? Like seriously does it feel good to watch us all cry? It's obvious you get off on it. You must do, because I sure as hell can't see any other reason as to why you'd do this to us. You're a bully; a big fat bully. Evil. And do you know what? I fucking hate you. I wish you were dead. I wish you would die; and I want it to be painful- like I want you to get cancer or something. I don't know how Tom copes with it, or mum. Because I can't anymore. I hate you.

The lights change.

CHRIS
You told her that from now on you have no sister? Unbelievable.

TAMMY
You think it's funny? I don't think that you're aware how hurtful and upsetting this is for me.

CHRIS
No Tam I don't think it's funny at all. I think it's sad. She's your sister.

TAMMY
And I reminded her of that.

CHRIS
Before or after you said you wouldn't accept her husband?
POLLY enters and sees TOM'. She takes a deep breath.

TOM
So she finally comes home.

POLLY
You normally work until eight on a Thursday?

TOM
I thought I'd come home and surprise you. Did you not think I'd be worried?

Beat. POLLY looks at TOM. She looks away.

You don't seem very happy about me being back.

POLLY
No, it's not that - it's just that -

TOM
You would have preferred me to be out until after nine? Yeah?

POLLY
No, it's just that - well um I was going to make us dinner-

TOM
Yeah, that would have been nice - but you know, it's alright; you had more important things to do I guess. Like the hoovering - nice job there babe.

POLLY
I did that yesterday and I didn't need-

TOM
Well I had a shower yesterday Polly. Doesn't mean I shouldn't do it today.

POLLY gives a nervous chuckle.

POLLY
Tom, I'm sor-

TOM
You just don't consider that I worry about you Pol. Anyway where were you? Not sure about that blouse babe.

POLLY
I went for coffee - with...Anna.

TOM
Great. How is the little gossip pot? She pronounced her undying love for you yet - what is it with you and your obsession with lesbians? I'm pretty hungry you know. Babe you could have at least got dinner ready.

POLLY
Tom I'm sorry.

POLLY touches TOM's hand. He pulls it away.

TOM
Polly, are you getting me?

She looks at him. Not entirely sure what to do.

Get. In. There. Stupid bitch.

She scurries into the kitchen.

The focus shifts to SIOBHAN. She has been crying. SHELLY enters.

SHELLY
Hey.

SIOBHAN
Hi.

SHELLY
You were crying when you came in. I thought I'd do the sister thing and see what's up.

SIOBHAN
I'm fine.
She begins to cry again.
Bloody men eh?

SHELLY
What's he done now? Same old?

SIOBHAN
It was different this time Shelly. He was different, it actually scared me a bit. But now I'm replaying it and trying to work out whether it's the fact that it was a proper argument that scared me. I don't know if I was actually scared of him or the fact that he could just end it. You know what I mean?

SHELLY
Is he worth this? Shiv seriously look at you.

SIOBHAN
Oh, thanks.

SHELLY
No, you know that's not what I meant Siobhan. Come on, come and have some dinner. Maybe "Bridesmaids" and some popcorn? Will that cheer you up?

SIOBHAN
I just wish I knew where I stood. He doesn't let me into anything. I've tried to get hold of him tonight and he's not replied; I feel like a stalker, I've double text him for god sake - he refused to meet mum and dad and yet he swears blind he doesn't wanna lose me. How can it feel so naughty and secret, but at the same time feel so genuine and make me feel like ours is the only relationship in the world? Where do I stand?

Focus shifts to TAMMY & CHRIS. They are sat in the bar.

TAMMY
I just want her to be safe Chris. She needs protecting.

CHRIS
Well, that's what he thinks isn't it?

TAMMY
So now you're saying I'm like him?

CHRIS
No Tammy - I - anyway - how can you protect her if you're not in her life?

TAMMY
Then you agree. She needs to be protected.

CHRIS
I didn't say that- but ask yourself the question. How can we help if we're out of her life?

TAMMY
So what do I do? Smile nicely at Tom and hope that he's not beating her?

CHRIS
If it means that you'll be in her life to protect her if things go wrong- then yes.

TAMMY
So you think it will happen again? You think something will go wrong?

CHRIS
We have to do this. For her. We just need to find a different tactic.

TAMMY
For goodness sake Chris - fine.

CHRIS
Tell her they're still welcome on Saturday.

TAMMY
I just don't want him in front of all of our friends.

CHRIS
Tammy - the man knows how to turn on the charm. You adored him when they first got together.

TAMMY
Oh god. Fine. I'll text her.

We shift back to POLLY & TOM.

POLLY
I've put the lasagne in. It shouldn't be too long.

TOM
I'm not really feeling lasagne tonight, but I guess you've put it in now; so...

POLLY
Oh you said this- I can put something else in?

TOM
Forget it babe. What's this crap you're watching?

POLLY
Home and Away -

TOM
Well I'm sick of it. Every night you watch this shit.

POLLY
Tom, I was watching that.

TOM
Well now you're not.

They sit in silence. She wants to talk but is worried about his reaction.

POLLY
Tom - listen, I -

Throughout the next section of dialogue, TOM constantly talks over her; making mimicking and stupid noises.

TOM
Come on baby spit it out.

POLLY
I had a visit from someone today.

TOM
What? Your other man?

POLLY
No, it's someone that hasn't been in our life for a while and I just had to get it off my chest and tell you and -

TOM
Oh great. Well are you gonna tell me or are we gonna play a guessing game?

POLLY
It was Tammy. She just text me as well and she wants us - me and you; to go to her birthday party on Saturday.

TOM
What? Why?

POLLY
I guess she just wants to make amends.

The focus shifts.

SHELLY
Tell him. Literally, give him two choices. He takes things seriously or its over. That's the only way to get any real commitment from him Shiv.

SIOBHAN
What if I lose him Shell? I really lo...like him. I really like him.

SHELLY
I've never seen you like this before. I tell you what- he upsets you again; you send him to me. Remember James Hutchinson?

SIOBHAN
Thanks Shelly.

The lights come back up on SIOBHAN & TOM's living room.

TOM
So, what - she popped round today out of the blue for a little visit?

POLLY
Yes. Well, no - she left me a voicemail last night.

TOM
Right, so she left you a voicemail?

POLLY
Yeah, but I-

TOM
And you didn't think to tell me?

POLLY
No, because I ignored it like we agreed we would.

TOM
And then she comes round today, to what - convince you to leave me?

POLLY
Tom, that's not fair, she's my sister and she cares ab-

TOM
She is a poisonous woman.

POLLY
Tom, please - she wants to be back in our life.

TOM
Yeah, she wants to be back Polly - but I don't think she wants to be back for decent reasons at all. Honestly - after all this time you think she just wants to pick up the pieces? Oh no - I don't think so baby.

POLLY
Tom, please, lets just go on Saturday and see if we can try and work out what she-

He suddenly grabs her face.

TOM
I said no Polly.

POLLY
But she-

TOM
Do you really want to argue about this again?

Focus crosses to TAMMY & CHRIS.

TAMMY
She's not going to come after today is she?

CHRIS
Oh come on, you've only just sent it!

TAMMY
It says she's read it.

CHRIS
This morning probably knocked her for six. Just let it sink in.

TAMMY
He's reacted badly. I know it.

CHRIS
Tammy.

TAMMY
Chris- I know, I can feel it.

CHRIS
No, Tammy we need to stop thinking like this! We said we'd stop this. What did I say about different tactics?

TAMMY
I can't. I can't just switch it off. I'm going mad with worry and I only sent the text ten minutes ago. I can't let him do this to her again.

TOM has his back to POLLY.

POLLY
Tom, please.

TOM
Don't you see? She's trying to make a joke of me Polly. She wants to get into our heads. Worm her way in and get close to us again, twist things and rip us apart.

TOM starts to walk towards POLLY and she is backed into the wall.

TOM
Polly, I'm just trying to protect us. I'm trying to protect us baby, protect you. You know how fragile you are baby; you don't want to be controlled. You don't need her controlling your life.

POLLY
But we wanted this didn't we, we wanted her to accept -

TOM
Oh Polly, she's not making you happy now is she? Is she making you happy? She's not making you happy.

She looks at him. Not sure what to say. She knows he could blow up at any point.
Oh wow. She's really got you wrapped round that little finger of hers again hasn't she? She's done it already hasn't she? She's already bloody done it again; this quickly. You know what- I bet she's sat over there on her high horse laughing away, cackling away whilst we're here struggling. We're struggling Polly.

POLLY
Struggling - I don't understand Tom? She just-

TOM
You don't understand? What is there to not understand Polly? She's trying to stupefy me. She's obsessed with me. She's manipulated you so that we argue, argue and struggle- struggle and doubt me, doubt me and hurt me. You just don't care do you? No - no you don't do you? See it's times like this I think to myself I should walk out the fucking door!

He has momentarily lost control and thrown her to the floor. She struggles onto her back.

POLLY
Tom, / please - please don't do this. Please Tom.

TOM
See that?! She's in - she's bloody in. She's in. Look what she's done to you. Look what she's doing to us.

POLLY
I haven't done / anything.

TOM
Oh yeah, that's about right. This place is fucking filthy.

POLLY
But I've tidied up.

A light comes up on HARRY.

HARRY
I didn't mean to make a mess.

TOM
You know it makes me wonder why we really are together if you're gonna take sides with that twisted sister of yours when you know how much she hates me. I mean how long is it since you last spoke to her Polly? Where's she been eh?

A spotlight comes up on SIOBHAN.

SIOBHAN
Firstly, I'm sorry about today. I shouldn't have been as rude and as forceful as I was. But do you know what? I believe in us Tom. I believe we can get somewhere - I believe in you. I know you're probably busy because you haven't answered your phone tonight, or responded to my texts and - I mean, that's fine. I'm not checking up on you, but I - but please, can I see you tomorrow? I'll meet you somewhere and we can chat. We can sort this out. I just need to know where I stand - I need to know what you want. Please ring me back.

TOM is backing POLLY again up against the wall. He is almost psychotic.

TOM
Don't let her do this to you Polly.

POLLY
Tom, Tom please.

TOM
Please what Polly?

POLLY
Tom- let me go.

TOM
I can't let you go Polly, I can't let you go. I worry about what you might do.

POLLY
Worry about what I might do?

TOM
You might get into trouble Polly, now that you don't think I'm worth listening to or caring about - I don't know if you can be trusted.

POLLY
You're scaring me.

TOM
You don't think you're scaring me?

POLLY
What?

TOM
Look at you; lying, full of stupidity, uncaring, you've become a slob, Polly you don't take any care of your appearance anymore. Lazy, rude - what kind of mother would you be?

POLLY
Tom, you're really scaring me.

TOM
How could a stupid, lazy woman like you cope with a baby? I wouldn't trust you with a baby, in fact I wouldn't trust you with a pig and that's your own kind, let alone a baby! I can't believe you want a baby.

He is gradually throughout this outburst poking at her face and her head. She snaps and pushes him away.

POLLY
No Tom! No, I am not lazy. Why do you think it's ok to speak to me like this? Have you actually considered what it feels like for me? I go day to day wondering how you're going to be when you get home from work - are we going to laugh? Are you going to be sarcastic and snarky all evening or are you going to go all out and be a complete fucking arsehole? I'm not lazy - I make sure that this house is perfect for you. I can't, I can't, it's - I mean for fuck sake Tom; I am on anti-depressants and I have been for months; didn't know that though did you? Because have you ever stopped to ask me if I was OK? I can't do this- I- this is- and you're the one who wants a baby! And I can't I can't -

He snaps. He slaps her. All that can be heard are the sounds of her sobs.

Lights up on HARRY & POLLY. They sit and in a choreographed movement both compose themselves after what has happened. Almost like a ritual they both go through the motions; stop crying, fix their clothes, feel their faces for marks, get up, put on a brave face, take a deep breath and leave the room.

It is late. TOM enters.

TOM
I love you.

POLLY
I know you do.

TOM
I didn't mean to hurt you. I was just - I was just shocked; I didn't realise that you felt like this. I didn't - I never mean to hurt you Polly; I just don't-

POLLY
But you do. You hurt me Tom.

TOM
Is it me?

POLLY
What?

TOM
Do I make you unhappy?
He begins to tear up.
Because I couldn't - I couldn't live with myself knowing that, that the only thing I love-

POLLY
I don't...no, no, it's not you. It's - I don't know. I don't know what it is Tom.

She breaks away and stands up, she moves across the room. He watches her. Sincerely. He considers.

TOM
Look, maybe it's the Tammy thing. I'm not - I'm not slagging her off; I just - look - I - it might help - why don't we maybe go to your sister's party?
She turns back to him.

POLLY
Do you mean that?

TOM
Yeah - if she lays off, then yeah. When is it?

POLLY
This Saturday. Thank you. This means so much to me.

TOM
I know.

He kisses her.

TOM
I love you.

POLLY
I love you too.

TOM
We need to make you get better. My fragile flower.

POLLY
You're my everything.

They kiss very passionately.

TOM
Lets go to bed eh?

Spotlights beam on SHELLY and TAMMY.

SHELLY
Dylan, open the/ door please.

TAMMY
Come outside. I need you to/ come outside.

SHELLY
It may seem bad, it may feel like you're/ on your own.

Between a Man and a Woman & *F*ckingLifeMate*. *The Plays of Scott James.*

TAMMY
I know you think that what I am saying isn't helpful and is well, quite ludicrous. But please.

BOTH
Let me in.

Beat.

SHELLY
I know what it feels like when you're trapped. Trapped. Trapped and fighting against something that has a horrible, dirty, black, hold on you. You feel like you have no one. That you are no-one. But this is the way you're being controlled.

TAMMY
Do you know what it feels like to see you disappear before my eyes? I feel like we're at sea, you've fallen overboard and I'm watching you drown. You're at sea, you're sinking, you're being tossed and thrown in the water. And I just can't get to you.

SHELLY
It probably seems really easy, doesn't it? To shut the people who love you out. But that's just because it's got under your skin. But please remember - you are not alone. There's tons of people out here who love you. Who want you back. Who want the Dyl, we love and know back.

TAMMY
I keep having this recurring nightmare. You know, that you've fallen overboard. You're in the sea, and I can't get to you. I can't get to you. You're drowning, I see the colour going from your face as the waves throw you around like a rag doll. We search everywhere for you, and we can't find you. And then, eventually we anchor up on the beach. I see this lifeless body and I run, I run as fast as I can. I run so fast that I keep falling over and I begin to swallow sand; but it seems unimportant and you're there. I get to you, and I try and pull you up. But you can't move. I try mouth to mouth, I try and pump your chest. But it doesn't work. I look at you, and you're bruised and battered. You're dead. I cry, I scream and no matter what I do- it does nothing.

SHELLY
I know that a film, and popcorn may not solve this. But I won't stop until I know you're OK again. Please Dylan. I love you.

TAMMY
Polly - please. I just wish you could see. I'm so scared that the only way that you'll leave this house is in a box.

Lights up on POLLY, she looks at TAMMY.

POLLY
Tammy - we'll be there tomorrow night.

TOM & SIOBHAN enter.

SIOBHAN
I just want to know where I stand Tom.

TOM
I don't want to lose you Shiv.

SIOBHAN
Then please, just meet them. Meet them once and then if it's not right then we'll take it slower. I just want some guarantee that you are now in this for the long run.

TOM
Man you don't let up do you? Look - I'm sick of this discussion I -

SIOBHAN
Yeah so am I. Forget it. You're just a waste of my time.

She goes to leave but he grabs her.

TOM
Look - OK! I'll meet them. I'll meet your parents.

SIOBHAN
Idle promises, here we go.

TOM
Alright call them now. As soon as you're free I can meet them.

SIOBHAN
Tomorrow.

TOM
Tomorrow? Look tomorrow I've....fuck it, alright lets do it tomorrow.

SIOBHAN
Do you mean it?

TOM
Yeah I mean it.

SIOBHAN
Oh Tom!

She kisses him across the table.

TOM
If it really means that much to you then who am I to disappoint you?

The lights focus on POLLY & TOM in separate locations on the stage.

POLLY
It was cold - well, I wouldn't say cold. Chilly. I had to wear a hat and a jacket. It's funny isn't it? How you can remember things like that.

TOM
I was so hot I thought I was going to pass out. I think it was because I was so nervous. I'd never ever been in a situation like this before.

POLLY
You were sweating. I loved it when you'd sweat - it was always because you were nervous about something or you were worried about something. It almost felt like - I don't know - it's silly - I kind of felt like I could see through to your soul. Whenever you sweat, your eyes get bluer, and I can feel whenever you look at me you want me there by your side. It makes me feel safe. I feel like I could stay in your arms stare into your eyes forever.

TOM
That hat. It looked far to big on your head. I think you'd taken it from the glovebox in my car. So I think the hat was probably mine. It's funny - whenever I'd sweat you used to look at me with this look in your eyes - this look that just eased me and made me feel safe. I don't think anyone else has ever been able to do that to me with the way they looked at me.

POLLY
You'd brought me up to this lake, somewhere in the valleys on our way to that mini-break you surprised me with on the way to Cardiff. When we got out of the car and I could feel the wind hit my face and you just held me. Held me tight. You looked at me, with your sweaty face. And you kept saying something like "I've been thinking and ummm, well umm"

Between a Man and a Woman & F*ckingLifeMate. The Plays of Scott James.

TOM
The thing is - I can't really. I don't know how to -

POLLY
"Just say it Tom!" I knew it. I knew it was coming. The moment we stepped out that car, and you held me and you were sweating. That was it. I just needed you to say it and then suddenly everything that happened with Mum and Dad would be OK. "Just say it Tom!"

TOM
And then I just said it. "Fuck it! Will you marry me Polly?"

POLLY
I think you got a nose bleed when I jumped at you.

TOM
I think you may have bust my lip.

POLLY
That's funny isn't it?

The lights change. POLLY is pacing.

POLLY
Oh god, Tom it's late.

She hears the front door slam. She sighs with relief. He walks in. He's drunk.

POLLY
I was worried about you. Glad you're home now, maybe now I can sleep- I'm shattered.

TOM
Alright Polly. I'm glad you're up, because...I think I'm owed something.

POLLY
Tom, have you been drinking?

TOM
I'm doing something very special for you. So you can do something special for me.

POLLY
Oh Tom, look I'm tired tonight. It's not a great time if you know what I mean.

TOM
Perhaps I wasn't making myself clear Polly. I wasn't asking.

POLLY
Not tonight Tom I'm really not feeling well, you know what I mean?

TOM
I won't say it again.

POLLY
No Tom, not tonight.

TOM
Come on, don't say no to me. I want it.

Something changes in Tom. He is very calm but it is exceptionally forceful - he kisses her neck and with force moves her to the floor it is not overly aggressive, but with great purpose and force. She squirms and tries to gently stop him as he climbs on top of her. She begins to move more uncomfortably and tries to assertively tell him 'no'.

POLLY
No Tom, please, no, please Tom, stop.

TOM
(At the same time as POLLY) Yes Polly, yes, yes, yes.

He grabs her and puts his hands over her mouth. He has lost his cool a little but has not reached an overly aggressive manner as their previous argument. She is beginning to cry - the horror setting in that he is not going to stop. He has undone his trousers.

TOM
Shut up, be quiet.

She cries and he kisses her neck, he enters her. She cries out in pain. HARRY stands behind them. He is upset.

HARRY
Please. Please open the door. I need to come in - I don't want to be in there on my own. Please. Look - I - please. Is what happened to me last night normal? It was meant to be 'special'. An act of love. I didn't feel loved. I felt dirty and it didn't feel like something you would do if you loved someone. I just need to know - has it happened to you? Are

you special. Please. Please. Please open the door. Please - I'm in pain. Tom, please open the door.

POLLY lays there, completely still, her hand on her mouth. She is horrified.

TOM
See, we can start a family. Be a family. That's what you want Polly.

Lights up on POLLY.

POLLY
I think I got used to the beatings. I mean - they were never pleasant and I never knew when they were coming, but I was never surprised when it happened. It had become something that was part of our marriage and maybe I was able to convince myself that things were fine as it would happen and then sure as hell you'd be 'you' again, we'd make love and everything would be nice for a while. But that...that night - I told you 'no'. I told you to stop. I couldn't believe it. You climbed on top of me and at first I struggled - I told you to stop but you didn't. You kept going and when I realised you weren't going to stop and I couldn't stop you - it felt like somebody had grabbed the top of my spine and snapped it. I couldn't move. I was paralysed with fear and you just kept going. It was hurting. It was aggressive. I think the worst thing about it was that you grabbed my face and pushed it away from you - so that I wasn't looking at you. It didn't feel like love. You're meant to love me and yet you can't even look at me. I lie there. Still - waiting for you to stop. Waiting for the nightmare to finish - it feels like a lifetime. It feels like I'm drowning. I feel like I'm going to be sick. And then you finish. It's over. It's been so aggressive that even what you've left inside me is hurting. And then you tell me we're going to have a baby. Something inside me tells me I can't get rid of my pills yet.

The stage comes to life and we see The COMPANY continue their motifs of anxiety, excitement, anger etc..
A spotlight beams on HARRY & TOM. A commotion can be heard.

HARRY
Do you reckon he's drunk again?

TOM
Of course he's drunk again. Nothing changes.

HARRY
I hate this. Why can't we just leave?

TOM
Apparently it's not as simple as that.

HARRY
But if we went somewhere else then mum -

TOM
Where would we go Harry? We've got nowhere else to go, and- and then social services would get involved; we'd be split up and put into foster homes -

HARRY
Yeah but we can take care of ourselves.

TOM
No, we're both under sixteen Haz it doesn't work like that.

There is a crescendo in the commotion. HARRY puts his hands over his ears. TOM moves to leave, HARRY grabs his arm.

HARRY
Tom, don't.

TOM
I have to don't I? He won't stop otherwise.

HARRY tries to pull TOM back and TOM snaps - he pushes HARRY away.

TOM
Harry just get off! I can't just sit up here pretending this isn't happening. Now just put your headphones in or something.

He exits.

The light shifts to POLLY, she is anxious as TOM hasn't arrived home yet. TOM enters..

POLLY
Oh, there you are. Better get going soon - she said people were starting to arrive from 7.

TOM
Sorry?

POLLY
Tammy's birthday party?

TOM
Tonight?

POLLY
Of course it's tonight.

TOM
You told me it was next Saturday?

POLLY
No, I definitely didn't. It's tonight.

TOM
Baby, you definitely said Saturday the 20th.

POLLY
I just don't think I would have got that wr-

TOM
What, so you're calling me a liar now?

POLLY
Oh, Tom - I'm not calling you a liar-

TOM
Yeah, well you told me it was next Saturday and now you're being really attacking when you've made the mistake.

POLLY
No, I'm not being attacking - I just really thought I told you it was tonight.

TOM
Well the thing is, you don't even realise when you're getting like that. You just get really snarky and quite defensive. That comes across as attacking. Maybe those stupid mood pills are messing with your head.

POLLY
Tom, the tablets aren't doing that - I just thought that I -

TOM
You told me it was next Saturday.

POLLY
Right. Well, no it's tonight.

TOM
Well then I can't go.

POLLY
What?

TOM
Yeah, I've got a work do uptown.

POLLY
But Tom you promised. You promised me and I promised Tammy and-
TOM
I know Polly but, you know, we all make mistakes and had you told me the right date, then this wouldn't be an issue.

POLLY
I'll go alone then.

TOM
What?

POLLY
I'll go on my own. You said that it might help me if I went and actually I don't see why I should miss my sisters birthday party.

TOM
No Polly, because if you go without me how do you think that will look to your sister?

POLLY
Tom - I haven't seen her properly in a year. I'll just explain that you forgot about something else.

She goes towards him and he puts his hands on her face- softly.

TOM
No you won't. Do you think your sisters sick mind will believe that?

POLLY
Tom please.

TOM
Polly, the woman's not well. She's mentally ill. She twists everything.

POLLY
Tom, she won't; yeah she'll be disappointed you're not -

TOM
I'm fairly certain she's borderline personalities, if not multiple. She's obsessed with me. I mean are you sure she's not jealous of us? You need to think about her wellbeing here too. I mean if you have mental problems then you probably get them from her. Me not being there will suddenly turn into a million different things. Our marriage will be in trouble, I don't want to see her, I'm cutting you off from your family. I mean how many times has she thrown that one at you before? I mean look what she did to us the other night. That argument we had was all brought on because of her and the things she'd put in your head.

POLLY
Tom, I really, really want to go.

TOM
You need to stand by me here Polly. This is a test. She is testing you.

POLLY
No, Tom this is stupid - she's not testing us.

TOM
I am your husband Polly. Or have you forgotten the vows we took?

POLLY
Please Tom.

Knowingly or not - he begins to press harder on her face.

TOM
Please what Polly? Please let go; *(mocking her)* Please let go Tom. I can't believe you, you really are ridiculous, you are SO selfish.

POLLY
How am I sel-

TOM
Here we are, selfish, self-centred Polly doesn't even know what she's done. Do you really not know what you've done?

POLLY
No, I don't, I don't under-

TOM
You are willing to make a laughing stock out of me, out of your husband, who you took vows with. You seem to just think I'm a joke these days. Is that it? Am I a joke to you Polly?

POLLY
No you're not, Tom please you're not.

TOM
Well that is what you will do if you go to this party tonight.

He pushes harder on her face.

POLLY
Ok Tom, please, no I won't- Tom - please let go you're really hurting me.

He bites her neck. She pulls away in pain.

TOM
That is how much you hurt me.

POLLY
Tom please let me go, she's my sister. Tom please, please.

TOM
Remember what I said - I'm your husband Polly. You stand by me.

He exits.

There is a knock at the door. SIOBHAN comes rushing to the door.

SIOBHAN
Shelly he's here. SHELLY!

SHELLY
Alright. Calm your tits.

SIOBHAN
Hi.

TOM
Alright. You look great.

SIOBHAN
Oh, it's just something I threw on.

SHELLY enters.

Tom, Shelly, Shelly, Tom.

TOM
Hey.

SHELLY
Hello Tom - nice to finally meet you; I've heard so much about you.

TOM
Ha - all good I hope.

They stand awkwardly for a moment.

SIOBHAN
I'm gonna run to the toilet very quickly before we go. (*Whispers to SHELLY*) Be nice.
She exits.

TOM
God - I feel so nervous.

SHELLY
I bet; getting in quite deep now.

TOM
Yeah; been a long time since I've done this...so Siobhan says you like popcorn?

SHELLY takes a leap of faith.

SHELLY
Cut your shit. You're married aren't you?

TOM
Excuse me?

SHELLY
What else could it be? The secret meetings, only meeting in central, reluctance to meet her family in fact at one point completely refusing to see it as anything other than a fling after five months.

TOM
Now that's a big assumption to make.

SHELLY
I know a slime ball when I see one.

TOM
You wanna think about who you're talking to -

SIOBHAN re-enters.

SIOBHAN
We ready?

TOM
Oh I'm more than ready to leave Shiv.

SIOBHAN
See you later Shell.

SHELLY
Bye, have fun.

TOM
Charming sister you have.

Shift to POLLY who is like a naughty child who could get scolded at any moment.

POLLY
Yeah, hi, umm I'd like to book a taxi please.

POLLY looks at TOM, who walks towards her. The ensemble block his path and lift POLLY away from him. Lights change. TOM is the middle of POLLY & SIOBHAN; both rotate around him and stop, showing various signs of tenderness- kissing, em-

bracing, sexual acts. With SIOBHAN it is tender and passionate, with POLLY aggressive.
The lights come up on SIOBHAN & TOM outside her parents.

SIOBHAN
Well here we go. They're going to love you.

TOM
God, I hope so.

SIOBHAN
They will. I know they will.

She kisses him. The focus shifts to POLLY, she is also stood outside TAMMY's house. She is pacing.

POLLY
Come on Polly, you can do this - you can do this. It's your sister; only your sister.

CHRIS comes out.

CHRIS
Polly!

POLLY
Chris - hi.

CHRIS
Is Tom parking?

POLLY
Um no, um Tom sends his apologies, but he's got a work do tonight uptown.. It's my fault, I gave him the wrong date by mistake. He's gutted he can't be here.

CHRIS
Ah well, the important thing is you're here Polly.

POLLY
It's good - really good to see you.

CHRIS
Come on, lets go in and let Tammy know you're here.

POLLY
Does she still wear Chanel?

They enter the house. TAMMY sees POLLY from across the room.

TAMMY
Polly! I'm so happy you're here.

POLLY
Tammy I -

TAMMY
Where's Tom?

POLLY
Oh he -

TAMMY
We really want to sort this Polly and he's fighting us every step of the way.

POLLY
No, he has a work do.

TAMMY
Tell you to say that did he?

POLLY
No it's true.

TAMMY
He just can't stand to face this.

POLLY
No Tammy. He's got a work do and even if what you say is true; could you blame him? I've been here less than thirty seconds and you've already launched an attack at him. Why can't you just stop misjudging him and saying hateful things about him that aren't true?

CHRIS has stood behind POLLY looking directly at TAMMY and has been signalling for her to stop. She finally takes notice.

TAMMY
You're right. I've had a drink and you know what I'm like when I've been drinking; I'm very glad you're here.

POLLY is overcome with guilt and emotion at the fact that she is seeing her family properly for the first time in a while, also the realisation has hit her that she has betrayed TOM. She is overcome with emotion as CHRIS is talking but tries to cover it. CHRIS notices.

CHRIS
Polly? Are you OK?

POLLY
Yeah, I'm fine - I just- just give me a moment.

She moves away. TAMMY has walked back over.

TAMMY
Polly - I didn't mean to -

CHRIS
Leave her - give her a moment to herself.

POLLY stands in the garden. She composes herself. HARRY who has noticed her earlier on throughout the party approaches her.

HARRY
Polly?

POLLY turns around and sees HARRY. She stops dead, she doesn't know what to do.

You alright? You look like you've seen a ghost. Not that scary am I?

POLLY
No...um, no, of course not. I just - what are you doing here?

HARRY
My girlfriend works with Chris - I didn't know that until we got here tonight.

POLLY
Oh, right. Umm - that's...small world...

HARRY
Where's Tom?

POLLY
Oh, a work do- he- he- forgot about...

She trails off and they stand in silence.

HARRY
I can't even think when I last saw you both.

POLLY
I don't know - your, um, your aunt's funeral maybe? Look - I'm a bit -

HARRY
It'd be nice if he answered my messages once in a while.

POLLY
Yeah - well, you know what Tom's like.

HARRY
I know he's happy with you, and that's a lot more than he's ever been - I guess ever, really.

POLLY shifts awkwardly. She looks at HARRY, not sure what to say.

POLLY
He...makes me happy too.

TAMMY comes bounding out

TAMMY
Here they are! What a small world eh?

TAMMY goes over to JOSH.

I always thought you were the cuter brother.

POLLY
Ok Tammy how much have you had?

TAMMY
Cheeky cow its my birthday- it's what I'm supposed to do; get horrifically drunk. Oh Linda is looking for you Harry.

POLLY
Oh, thanks. I mean, right. Well I'm pretty tired and I better -

HARRY
I tell you what we're gonna pop round soon; haven't seen that brother of mine in ages. It'll be great to catch up with you both.

POLLY
Well - Tom's really busy at work and he's not got much time.

HARRY
It'd be nice if he made time for me.

POLLY
It was lovely seeing you both.

She hastily makes an exit. TAMMY follows her grabs her.

TAMMY
Polly - thank you.

POLLY
For what? I didn't do anything.

TAMMY
Yes you did. You came tonight - and that means a lot.

POLLY
I wouldn't have missed it for anything.

TAMMY
I'm sorry for what I said about Tom.

POLLY
He wants everything to be OK again Tammy. He just doesn't know how to.

TAMMY
I love you and I'm so proud of you whatever happens.

They smile at each other and hug.

Lights up on SIOBHAN & TOM cramped in her single bed.

SIOBHAN
You certainly know how to turn on the charm that's all I'm saying.

TOM
And you certainly have a small bed. Do you think they liked me?

SIOBHAN
They loved you Tom.

TOM
If that's what makes you happy, then I'm happy.

SIOBHAN
I love you.

He kisses her. The lights fade. POLLY appears.

POLLY
Tom?

TOM
Polly?

POLLY
Please Tom.

TOM
Polly - I -

SIOBHAN stands up.

SIOBHAN
This is ridiculous- you need to decide what you want/, because I don't know if you're even sure yourself. This is absurd. We've never been in a completely private location together. Don't. Don't tell me that the hotels are private. Yes, maybe we aren't with other people, but it's still in a neutral location. Neither of our homes. Now as much as I've loved the hotels and I say loved because even properly spending time together is now a thing of the past, it's just got seedier and dirtier because these days I just come here for a quickie.

POLLY
The moment you took me to that cute little restaurant down some little country lane in Sevenoaks, I knew I wanted to spend the rest of my life with you - you looked into my eyes and I saw a beautiful person that I had the hugest love for. I remember the first time you held me; I thought I could stay there forever. So strong, safe, sure. Sweet, so sweet - everything you did you did because you cared. But now, you hurt me. You hurt me Tom.

TOM is becoming agitated and struggling to split his attention between the two.

TOM
What am I doing? I have a wife at home who loves me, you know she'll do anything for me. She stopped her passion; she stopped writing because I couldn't bare her to focus on anything but me. She stays with me every time, every time I've hurt her. I love her so much though and I just don't know why I do it. I can't control it - it just takes hold and I want to control something - her I just -

POLLY
Tom, Tom please. Stop Tom, please, please Tom, please.

The COMPANY begin to surround TOM; the feeling becomes nightmarish. All of his demons are represented. Sex, anger, abandonment, jealousy. TOM screams. The COMPANY fall to the floor. TOM gradually throughout this has began to suffocate himself. He falls to the floor. Crying. The COMPANY begin to rewind and circle TOM. He jumps out of his skin.

SIOBHAN
You ok baby?

TOM
(Jumping) Yeah, I just had a weird...um fucking weird dream. Go back to sleep, I'm just gonna grab a glass of water and then I'll be back to bed.

The lights fade again. The lights change, we realise it's morning. SHELLY appears in front of TOM.

SHELLY
Going home to the wife are we?

TOM
You don't know what you're talking about.

SHELLY
I'll get her to see you for what you really are.

He gets close to her and whispers.

TOM
Is that so? She loves me, and she won't believe a word that her jealous, single sister says. Ruin this and you'll be sorry. I'll be impressed that you've achieved the impossible, but you'll be sorry.

He leaves.

SHELLY
What a wanker.

The lights shift.

HARRY
Can I tell you something? I struggle to trust anyone in relationships really. It scares me - my last girlfriend Katy; I loved her. Like really, loved her. We were twenty and she got pregnant, and you know what I freaked out. I thought to myself; what if I'm like him- what if my little kid is born into a world where dad can't communicate any emotion other than anger and then guilt. I must have smiled as a kid - I must have, every kid smiles right, every kid laughs - but the few memories of good times I have; I realise now because my father was feeling guilty and as if he needed to make up for something. I thought about how my child would feel if I were that father. I freaked out. I couldn't do it - I had a nightmare that we lived in this little house; it was nice, you know like the house in Downton Abbey or something like that, and my son - he looked just me - and Katy, she was dressed to kill, like she looked amazing; not that she didn't in real life, but you know? We were eating dinner and someone said something, I can't quite remember what but I flipped. I was crying, screaming; I smacked Katy and I punched that child. I remember the anger so vividly. I looked in the mirror and all I saw was him. I woke up crying and I broke it off with Katy - she didn't understand why and I couldn't tell her. I wish I could have stayed but how could I live with myself if I let that happen? She had an abortion....and it was my fault...I was as bad as him. But you know what? Linda I'll tell you everything. Because I care about you - I really do and I want to be with you. You make me so happy - but I have to be honest about why I'm the way that I am. Because what if this were to happen again? That baby...man I still wonder, I wonder all the time - what they would have looked like. Boy or girl? Kind? Brave? Footballer or singer? It was all my fault.

LINDA
I don't know - I mean I've never experienced anything like what I imagine you've experienced. Not first hand anyway, but I remember - at home, when I was at school; there was this boy. He was a bit odd, quiet, aloof um a little eccentric - you know? Well he used to come into to school sometimes with battered lips and I dunno, I guess he just looked tired and sad - and I remember he'd be pulled out of class all the time by our school councillor and by teachers and anyone who was an important member of staff. And we always found it odd and I think one day someone asked him why he was always called out of class. But he always made up some excuse. Well - he killed himself. They found him...hanging in the woods. He'd left a note. The note said something about him not being able to be 'special' anymore, the burden was too much, or something like that. But - his dad had been abusing him. Sexually and maybe physically. And nothing had been done. His mother hadn't done anything - I guess she was too scared or I don't know maybe she didn't know. He was alone. Frightened and alone - and his only way out was to kill himself. I can't imagine it, being that isolated and that lonely that the only way out is to do that. I can't understand how you couldn't say anything to anyone in that situ-
HARRY has crumbled. He is in tears. He sobs.

Hey, hey - come on. What is...oh god Harry.

She holds him. He sobs into her.

I'm here. I'll always be here. It doesn't matter.

HARRY
It's fucking dirty. I never stop feeling dirty and I close my eyes at night and it's still happening. I hear a door creak and my heart stops. I'm never gonna escape it Linda. I'm never gonna be free. And it's the guilt - the way he'd buy presents or make you'd feel special or like it was something good. He's always gonna have me.

LINDA
Hey, stop it. We'll do this. We'll get through this together. We can take things as slow as you need. But don't ever bottle things up. You tell me - OK? I don't care how deep and dark we have to go. I love you and I'm gonna be here.

TOM sits alone. POLLY notices TOM and gently touches his shoulder. He jumps.

POLLY
You didn't come home last night.

TOM
Yeah I stayed in a hotel.

POLLY
It was lonely without you.

TOM
I'm really sorry Polly. I know I let you down.

He hands her a letter. She reads it.

POLLY
It's beautiful.

TOM
I shouldn't have swanned off uptown and left you here on your own knowing that your sister was having a party. I'm sorry.

POLLY
It's fine. I'm sorry too.

TOM
I love you, you know.

POLLY
Me too.

He kisses her.

TOM
What do you say we have a night off? How about we get a Chinese?

POLLY
Yeah. That's great.

TOM
Why don't you go out for the day? Call Anna go out for a walk round Bluewater or Lakeside?

POLLY
Yeah, I'll go and give Anna a ring.

TOM
I love you Polly.

POLLY
I love you. So much.

The lights shift. SIOBHAN & SHELLY are on separate sides of the stage.

SIOBHAN
For some reason my sister's always been insecure about me and men. She seems to be so angry and determined to ruin it when I meet someone. I don't know if it is jealousy or fear of losing me or because she's been hurt by men or whatever; but it's my life you know?

SHELLY
Yeah men have always screwed me over. I just don't want that happening to Siobhan. She's my sister for christ sake and I just want to protect her and keep her safe. She's my best friend, the person I trust with anything. But I just wish she didn't fall for such nob-ends.

The lights shift.

SIOBHAN
I mean you've said crap about last boyfriends Shell but this really takes the piss.

SHELLY
I'm not doing this to be mean or hurt you Shiv - just wouldn't it explain a lot?

SIOBHAN
But it would also mean that Tom has lied to me all this time and I don't believe that.

SHELLY
Why can't you see that he's got you wrapped round his little finger? You barely know anything about him and you have changed. You have changed a lot in the last five months.

SIOBHAN
You're just jealous you know- I mean which one of us has the boyfriend and who's been single for about three years?

SHELLY
Oh you cheeky little cow, when will you wake up to yourself? He threatened me.

SIOBHAN
What?

SHELLY
He told me that if anything went wrong between you two I would be sorry. He said he didn't need to worry about what a pathetic jealous sister had to say to you. He never denied he was married Shiv.

SIOBHAN
Yeah, well...I bet you provoked him.

SHELLY
Oh, you're talking bollocks Shiv.

SIOBHAN
Listen to yourself, no wonder you're single. You really are a contemptuous, spiteful little bitch.

SHELLY
Well look who's talking - Little Miss Stuck up; seriously "I think I'm the prettiest girl in school." Not to mention immature -

SIOBHAN
Well at least I'm not a chav.

SHELLY
Grow up Shiv! I can't believe you're being let loose to teach children next year.

SIOBHAN
Ugh - no wonder Dylan killed himself; if I had a girlfriend like you I'd kill myself too.

Both know that SIOBHAN has gone too far.

SHELLY
I can be a bitch sometimes though.

SIOBHAN
Sometimes I don't know when to stop.

The lights change and HARRY is sat in TOM & POLLY's living room with TOM.

HARRY
It's nice you've buried the hatchet with Tammy and Chris.

TOM
It's important to Polly and clearly that's what matters.

The front door slams.

TOM
That'll be Polly now.

POLLY enters. She sees HARRY and stops dead.

POLLY
Hi.

TOM
You didn't tell me you'd seen Harry at the party last night Polly?

POLLY
Yeah...it totally slipped my mind.

TOM
Yeah, I bet it did.

POLLY
It was lovely to see you Harry.

TOM
You know I am starving. We'll order that Chinese in yeah?

POLLY
I can go and get it if you want?

TOM
No. We'll order it in.

HARRY has noticed the tension.

HARRY
Well I better go.

TOM
See you later Haz.

HARRY gives POLLY a hug.

HARRY
Take care Polly. You know, Linda's great, I reckon you two would get on well. She's a good listener.

He goes to exit, turns around and makes the decision and leaves. The door slams. POLLY & TOM stand in complete silence.

TOM
Where did I specifically ask you not to go last night?

Silence.

TOM
Cat got your tongue?

He moves towards her, eventually grabbing her.
TOM
You deceitful little slut. What have you done? What is your sister going to think of us now? You fucking little liar!

POLLY
Tom, please- you're hurt-

TOM
Hurting you? Good cos I want to hurt you, I want to fucking hurt you Polly.

He throws her face down to the floor. He goes down to her level- grabbing her.

POLLY
Tom OK I went to the party. I'm sorry.

TOM
You completely betrayed me. You've pretty much told Tammy that everything she has done over our marriage is right. You've let her decide what happens in this marriage. You've betrayed me Polly.

POLLY
She's my sister.

TOM
She's manipulating you Polly, what part of you can't see she's manipulating you?! She's poison, a leach on our relationship.

POLLY
By doing what Tom? Telling me that you're hurting me? Telling me that you're stopping me from seeing my family? I love my sister so much and you know what? Last night when I went in that house I cried because I felt so guilty that I had gone when I know you needed me to stand by you. But I just couldn't help but feel happy, because she is my family. She tells me I should leave you.

He slaps her. He stands up, stifles a scream and composes himself.

You know, you say it's Tammy causing this depression. Well maybe it's you Tom. Maybe I should tell my counsellor about this - see if we can make some headway. I mean anyone being treated like this is going to end up screwed up aren't they?!

TOM attacks POLLY. He punches her in the stomach. She pushes him off and in retaliation, slaps him. He punches her clean to the floor. He attacks her again.

Blackout.

Spotlight on TOM.

TOM
Sometimes I get asked about the scars on my legs - if anyone sees them, I mean. I tell them I fell off a bike and fell onto a rockery. That's what I told you the first time you asked. But I was sweating, and you always knew when I was sweating that something had made me nervous. It was such a big thing to tell you that I had done that to myself. But I couldn't tell you why. How could I tell you what I went through? I didn't want anyone's pity. I didn't want you to love me because you felt sorry for me. It's funny though - I didn't do that to myself because of the physical things - you know, like the beatings or whatever. In some ways that actually meant something - because at least I was getting something. Mum walked out once. I couldn't have been any older than seven. I thought she was gone forever and I cried. I was so frightened - I think I was a bit of a mummy's boy if I'm honest. I kept asking where is she? "Dad where's mummy?" And he just ignored me, I kept crying until eventually he told me to grow up. "Stop crying. Boys don't cry. What are you, a little girl?" I was seven. I don't think me and dad ever had a proper conversation after that. Unless I was getting in-between him and mum or I was getting a beating for something. That was the only time we ever communicated. Harry was his favourite - yeah he got beatings, but he got presents, and he got attention and Dad wanted him. Dad liked seeing him. Dad even - I mean he couldn't even do that to me - he stopped once the hands were under the duvet and left the room. It was around that time that the cutting started. I mean how fucked up is that? That the fact that your little brother gets more attention than you by getting sexually abused is the reason you cut yourself.

Lights up on HARRY. He stands behind TOM.

HARRY
Tom...Tom pick up the phone. Whatever you're doing it's not worth it. I know that look Tom. Please, just call me back and please don't do anything stupid.

ANNA enters. POLLY has marks of 'X' on her face to signify bruises.

ANNA
So this is why you haven't answered my calls the past few days. I'll kill him.

POLLY
Anna, don't. What good will it do? I did exactly what he said not to do. And I paid for it. That's it.

ANNA
Polly - has the man manipulated you that much that you actually believe you deserved what happened to you last night?

POLLY
He just needs support and love. He needs someone to stand by him and look after him. He's had people let him down his whole life.

ANNA
It's your fault this is getting worst.

POLLY
Anna, what?

ANNA is very forceful in what she is saying.

ANNA
Yeah- you heard me right. This has got worst because you don't stop it happening. I mean, it's laughable that everyone tries to help you and get you out of this, and the thing is you can't see that they do it because they care. Maybe you enjoy it-

POLLY
Anna please -

ANNA
Because you know what I think will happen someday soon? I think I'm going to come round here and find you dead. I mean, why shouldn't I? You're not stopping it - Polly you are allowing this to happen!

POLLY
Tom loves-

ANNA
Tom loves you; yes, yeah maybe Tom does love you in some messed up way - but this - THIS; isn't normal and this isn't right. You have to stop this now - as this has already gone too far.

POLLY has broken down in tears. She cries for a few moments. ANNA holds her. Eventually POLLY composes herself.

POLLY
I know things are wrong Anna. I know something needs to be done.

ANNA
You've suffered in silence for far too long Polly.

POLLY
What can I do? I've got nothing Anna. I've lost pretty much everyone. He is the only person really in my life. Without him - I am broken. I don't know how to be anything without him anymore.

ANNA
You've got me and Mel. You've got your sister. You've just been made to believe that you are nothing - that you have nothing without him. That's his way of controlling you Polly.

POLLY
I don't know what to do.

An idea comes to ANNA.

ANNA
Why don't we go up to his office? Tell him that we're going out for lunch and we can talk things out with him.

POLLY
No. Absolutely not.

ANNA
Polly - I can sit there as your support and you can say everything you need to say to him. It won't happen otherwise. Plus if we're in a neutral location he's more likely to listen.

POLLY
No. The only person who will pay for that is me.

ANNA
No - you're going to come and stay with us for a while. I don't think you're safe in this environment anymore.

POLLY
I can't. Anna -

ANNA
Just trust me. Get your coat.

The lights fade.

SIOBHAN and TOM are in his office. The situation is fraught. TOM is on the phone.

TOM
Umm- no, it's. I'm a bit - it's..it's not a good time right now. Thanks.
He puts the phone down.

Go on. Keep going. Get it off your chest.

SIOBHAN
Tom, she's my sister. I don't appreciate threats being made to her.

TOM
Look are you sure she hasn't misunderstood me? I'd never threaten her - I barely know the woman.

SIOBHAN
I've seen you angry. The day you lost your temper with me. I can well believe you'd behave like that.

TOM
Look, I'll be honest with you Shiv. I'm having a bit of a dodgy time at the moment- things are hectic here, it's hard work and trying to juggle-

ANNA bursts in with POLLY followed by an ASSISTANT. There has been a noise proceeding this.

ANNA
And here he is, the champion woman beater. Why didn't you want to see us Tom?

ASSISTANT
I'm sorry Tom, I tried to stop them but they pushed straight past. She's mad.

TOM
It's fine, just, just get out.

A crowd has gathered outside the room upon hearing the commotion.

ANNA
No, let her stay - I want *everyone* to see what you've done.

SIOBHAN
Who are these people Tom?

TOM
Wait a minute Shiv.

ANNA
Shiv? This your little bit on the side Tom?

POLLY
Tom, no. Please, please don't...no.

SIOBHAN
I'm his girlfriend if that's what you mean? Who are you?

ANNA
A cheat as well as a woman beater.

POLLY looks at him in a disbelief. Suddenly she has an outburst.

POLLY
You bastard.

TOM
Polly please - it's not what it looks like.

POLLY
YOU BASTARD.

She walks through the crowd who are watching.

TOM
Get her back here.

He grabs ANNA.

TOM
Get her back here you dyke!

ANNA smacks him one.

ANNA
Stay away from Polly. She'll be gone when you get home.

She walks out. The crowd disperses. TOM turns and looks at SIOBHAN.

SIOBHAN
You did that to her?

She stands up and slowly walks past him. He stands alone. He runs out.

The lights come up on various points of the stage. Phones are heard ringing. The following dialogue overlaps.

TAMMY
Hi.

SHELLY
Hey.

TAMMY
Oh god - we'll be there as soon as possible.

SHELLY
Shiv - I'm so sorry.

TAMMY
But she's my sister- I want to help.

SHELLY
He's not worth these tears you know.

TAMMY
You're right - if I see him; I'll kill him.

SHELLY
I'll be home soon, then we can watch "Bridget Jones", eat popcorn and cry together, yeah?

TAMMY
Thank you Anna. Thank you for being there for her throughout all this.

SHELLY
I love you sis.

Lights up on SHELLY & SIOBHAN.

SIOBHAN
How could I be so stupid? I'm sorry for what I said the other day.

SHELLY
So am I.

SIOBHAN
I mean it Shell- what I said was unforgivable.

SHELLY
I sometimes wonder if it was me.

SIOBHAN
Oh my god Shelly no. Do you miss him?

SHELLY
Everyday. I mean it's got easier, of course it has, but not a day goes by when I don't think of him. You know, now I can think of him without crying, most of the time anyway, and I can think of him and smile. Smile at the happy days we had together. He was my Dyl and that will never, ever change.

SIOBHAN pulls SHELLY close.

SIOBHAN
Come here. Let's watch "Forgetting Sarah Marshall".

BOTH
Popcorn?

Lights come up on POLLY in their living room.

ANNA
(from outside) Let me in you bastard. Polly! POLLY!

TOM enters. He looks awful. They stand staring at each other. A separate light shines on HARRY. He stands in the corner of the room.

TOM
Look Polly - the thing is; you didn't let me explain at lunch today. That girl, she's, she's not who you think she is.

POLLY
Well she seemed to think so.

He walks closer to her and she moves away.

TOM
Polly listen to me -

POLLY
Tom, just tell the truth!...Please Tom, look what you've done to me. The least you can do is be honest.

TOM
I've been seeing her -

POLLY
How long?

TOM
Five months.

She crumbles.

POLLY
For christ sake. I'm leaving Tom.

She goes to leave and he grabs her arm.

Between a Man and a Woman & F*ckingLifeMate. The Plays of Scott James.

TOM
Come on Polly - we can sort this out.

POLLY
Sort out what Tom? Sort out the fact that I'm completely isolated - sort out the fact that I don't know who I am in the hours that I'm not with you? Sort out the fact that I don't see my family anymore? Sort out the fact that you use me as a punch bag? Sort out the fact that you go and sleep with a fucking teenager?! No Tom. Unlock this door Tom.

ANNA
Polly.

POLLY
Anna there's a key - get away from me Tom.

She walks back into the living room. TOM follows her.

TOM
We have plans - we wanna start a family.

POLLY
No Tom - you want to start a family. I have no choice in the matter like I have no choice in any other matter. I'll go out the back door.

He grabs her hand.

TOM
Polly you do not mean this.

She pushes him away, finally snapping.

POLLY
You controlled me!

A spotlight beams on HARRY. The next lines between HARRY & POLLY are almost delivered simultaneously.

HARRY
I wish you were dead.

POLLY
You are a sad, evil, controlling little man and I am not scared of you anymore Tom! I am not.

TOM
We love each other Polly, we're gonna have a family. A real family.

HARRY
You don't scare me anymore. Mum's scared but I don't see why I should be scared. Look at you.

POLLY
A baby; with you? No, I don't think so- so you can beat that when I can't take any more?

HARRY
Why don't you pull in one of your skanks to live with you? You can use her as a punchbag as well.

TOM
This isn't, we're gonna have a family. A loving family. You love me- I'm your husband.

POLLY
You know what - you can't really love me Tom. Why on earth would you do this to me if you loved me?

TOM
We are going to be a family.

She snaps. She screams.

HARRY
So go on, hit me. Hit me you cunt - that's all you'll ever be good for. Hurting someone; beating someone; touching someone - you're a nonce! How does that make you feel eh? So hit me - I know you're dying to! Go on.

POLLY *Overlapping HARRY*
We are not going to be a family! I NEVER CAME OFF THE PILL! And why do you think? I didn't - because you could never be a father! YOU ARE JUST LIKE YOURS!

TOM
YOU FUCKING BITCH. I AM NOTHING LIKE HIM!

TOM snaps- he punches POLLY to the ground. HARRY reacts as if he's been hit. A nightmarish sequence ensues. TOM goes to POLLY on the floor in his confusion, initially trying to apologise. He however ends up clawing at her neck. The COMPANY begin to become TOM's subconscious. The COMPANY repeat their various movements. Somebody climbs on top of HARRY as he struggles to get to POLLY & TOM.

HARRY
Stop, alright I'm sorry, please, please. I didn't - stop! DAD STOP! PLEASE DAD STOP!

ANNA comes in and tries to pull TOM off Polly - TOM throws her off - in her panic, she cries, desperately begging TOM to get off of POLLY. TOM raises his fist to punch POLLY clean in the face. She screams desperately.

POLLY
TOM!

He stops himself. Falling off of her, realising what he's about to do. He cries.

Blackout.

A spotlight beams on TOM.

TOM
Polly. Polly please don't leave me. I can't lose you. Polly please. I need you - we need each other. We're gonna have a proper family. Finally I'm gonna have a proper family. If you leave, I'm broken. Forever.

He begins to cry.

POLLY! I'm begging you please don't walk out my life. Don't shut me out.

Dad please, please dad. Just look at me - just listen to me. Why don't you want to talk to me? Why don't you wanna spend time with me? Please just talk to me! Just answer me. Call me names, call me a cunt, beat me - just give me anything. Why don't you wanna touch me? Why is Harry so special? Why am I just forgotten about? Why am I only good for a beating? Please Dad, just don't ignore me.

Please - someone. Please - don't walk out. I can't. I can't be on my own again.

SIOBHAN enters.

SIOBHAN
It's funny isn't it? The notion of owning someone. It's not a nice thought at all when you put it frankly. I own you. I decide what you wear, what you eat, how you think, who you talk to. No one should ever have that control, or be put in a position where they're allowed to think that. But isn't there something nice about someone saying to you "you're mine. I choose you. You. Above everyone else." But maybe they were wrong for each other. I bet nobody's asked him how he is. No one thinks of that. Maybe they didn't love in the right way and that's why he was confused by how to look after her. Maybe this is for the best.
She gets her phone out.

Tom, I- listen - if. Oh, it's Siobhan. Look I know there's a reason for everything that's happened and I, I know this is probably a very tough time. But. Umm. I'm here for you. I'm here and want to be there for you. Please get back to me Tom. I. I love you.

The lights change.
TAMMY
After all these years I've got my little sister back. She's happy.

CHRIS
How long is it before you accept that something isn't right and you walk away?

ANNA
Approximately two women a week die due to domestic violence. One in three will suffer in their lifetime. How long was it before Polly was just another figure?

HARRY
We promised we'd never be like him. That man ruined our childhood. He ruined mum's life. You turned into him and you can't even admit it.

TOM and POLLY face each other. Everybody else exits.

TOM
I know that I've treated you appallingly Polly. / I do and I hate myself.

POLLY
You think of prison as having big walls, bars on the windows, / barbed wire everywhere. But it's not always, is it?

TOM
I can't believe I allowed myself to become the very…My biggest fear in the world was turning into my dad. I mean - its ridiculous isn't it? I had the most horrific experiences and suffered with my mother and my brother at the hands of my father, and yet here I am - losing my wife because I've behaved the same way. It's all I know. I don't know how to treat someone a wife or a girlfriend or anyone really with kindness /, not for long anyway.

POLLY
I thought to myself "It must be me."

You broke me.

TOM
I remember one time, Harry snapped. He told dad everything that he'd done wrong over the years. By the time we'd managed to get dad off of him, he'd beaten him to a pulp. Literally. He had a broken nose, concussion and he lost four teeth - he was in hospital for a week, the doctor said he was one punch away from a coma…or death. And you know, I hated myself - because I had the tiniest twinge of happiness, because maybe now he wasn't so special anymore.

POLLY
You isolated me.

TOM
It's all I know. I don't know what a normal, happy relationship is; I never, ever saw one - I try, I tried so hard, but in the end you go back to what you know and what you've learnt.

POLLY
You beat me.

TOM
I don't know if it's in blood, like genetic or something or whether its just all I know.

POLLY
Tom - you raped me.

TOM
But I will regret what's happened for the rest of my life. You're the best thing that ever happened to me Polly and no matter what happens I will always love you, and I tried, but you can't blame me-

POLLY

POLLY begins to wipe off the marks on her face.

Tom...Now I live on my own in a one bedroom flat; it's nice coming and going as I please. I hope one day you're able to face your demons and get over them; that may be impossible, I don't know. But one thing is certain - I loved you, really loved you and I let you treat me like, I don't know what, but now I'm out and I'm never coming back - I can't be with someone who doesn't know how to love me. I'm stronger. I'm happy. You've given me these reasons and excuses. But I can't let myself buy it. Not this time.

She hands TOM back the wedding ring and walks away. TOM is left alone. Blackout.

F*ckingLifeMate

A play by Scott James

Between a Man and a Woman & F*ckingLifeMate. The Plays of Scott James.

F*ckingLifeMate was first performed at the Bread & Roses Theatre, London (UK), from 27th February to 10th March 2018. It was directed and produced by Scott James and presented with the following cast

KIRSTY
Kelsey Short

CASSIE
Chantal Richardson

CHELSEA
Samantha Jacobs

HAYLEY
Jasmin Gleeson

JORDEN
Roisin Gardner

BRADLEY
Nathan Lister

PETER
Michael Flanagan

Characters

KIRSTY

HAYLEY/MUM

JORDEN/NATHAN

CHELSEA/MISS LOCKLEY/NURSE/SINGER

PETER/DAD

CASSIE/STEVE

BRADLEY

*Note: This script went to print before the end of rehearsals and may vary slightly from that presented on stage.

KIRSTY enters. She stands on her own.

KIRSTY
It's funny isn't it? How people fall into the stereotypes of various things; your dad beats your mum, so you pick a guy that'll beat you within an inch of your life, seven days a week until you eventually leave him and end up with someone else and he'll eventually end up doing the same thing. Then your brother will becomes an emotional fuckwit, who will beat his wife. Or say your mum had you when she was thirteen, so you try and beat her record by having your kid when you're twelve and really beat her by having three kids by the age of fifteen. Well my story is a fucking cliché - and my family probably fall into all types of stereotypes. Stereotypes that in an election - one side would use as a reason for cutting benefits and making everything private and the other an example of how we need to improve our council system. Mum hits dad. It's not a classic damsel in distress story - no way mate. Mum hits dad first most of the time. We were learning about dysfunctional families in social science once in like year nine and in this book it said there was typically two types of volatile homes; ones where the kids have no idea that mum and dad are completely mental heads or where the kids get beaten as well. Well, that ain't the case for my family - I am fully aware that my dad can be a cunt. Like, literally can sometimes be the king of cunts. My mum is an even bigger cunt, and we were and always are fully aware of what's going on, but - we've never, ever been touched. Ever. Mum and dad have never put their hands on us; not even a smack for being naughty, or for the time I took a pair of size seven stilettos from Primark when I was four.

We were a typical dysfunctional, fucked up family. Lived in a shitty council estate in South East London. I watched an interview with Nicole Kidman - talking about how she grew up in Sydney, apparently "there were beautiful blue skies with a crystal clear sea. Breathing in the air was inhaling pure goodness and crime was non-existent" Blah, blah, wank, wank, wank. Fuck yourself. If you were to ask me to describe where I grew up, I'd have to tell you; in Thamesmead the sun never shines, it's always greyer than Theresa May's pubes and people would stab you soon as they would finger you. It's pretty much the face of campaign for "Broken Britain". You see people round this area- generations of people all blend into one. A vicious cycle in which each person sticks round the estate. Living off benefits. Getting pregnant as you leave school. In and out of prison. Yeah, we've got iPhones and laptops now; but we're still living in the exact same cycle as a couple of generations ago. It's funny - growing up, I always thought my parents were different. I remember, all my mates parents would be at home when they got home from school; and my mum and dad were hardly ever there. Not at the same time anyway. I used to wish that they didn't go to work and they'd be there like my friends parents. And like, now I realise they had to go to work, or else how would they support two snot balls? They didn't tick the right boxes or have enough wrong with them to rely on their benefits - which they didn't get much of. You're fucked if you do and you're fucked if you don't. You get a job that helps support you - it takes you over the threshold and you ain't entitled to benefits anymore; but the benefits ain't enough to cover you properly and neither is the job. What do you do in that situation - aside from just get stuck in the same rut day in, day out. Barely scraping by on the breadline, but viewed as some council scrounger cos there ain't no other way of getting by. Maybe the stress of that made them start taking pieces of out of each other? I wouldn't mind, but someone needs to remind them; a cuppa is for drinking, not throwing over someones face or the wall. Mad fuckers.

I wouldn't be the person I am without my mates though. Couldn't get by without them. And the good thing about it - is each one of them is as fucked up as me in their own own way. Apparently I'm the posh one of the group cos my parents are still together. Lucky me right? So we've got Chelsea.

CHELSEA enters.

Always in and out of internal exclusion. Came out as a lezzer this year and realised that the fact she was suppressing wanting a bit of fanny was causing her anger. So, now she's more focused on making a point that she's gay - this gives her something to focus her anger on and a protection mechanism- no one wants to be gay round here. They say we're in a more accepting world now; they obviously didn't grow up here. Then we've got Jorden.

JORDEN enters.

In the bottom set for everything because she's a thick bitch. Her GCSE predictions are lower than the Queen's tits; but she always gets by somehow, because she's really fucking pretty, under the fake tan- and also because her brother is shit scary; was in juvie at the age of thirteen, fifteen and then was back in prison by the time he was nineteen, had been in and out prisoner about four times - her family is the best example of getting stuck here. Got a bit of a name for himself around South East London. So taking the piss out of her wouldn't be a great idea...well, not to her face. Now, I don't really like to say I have a best mate - but if I'm being honest I'd have to say that Hayley was my best mate in the group.

HAYLEY enters.

She's a bit hard, but like, I get that; me and her, we have pretty similar homes. Her dad's an alcoholic - their home an get pretty volatile too. We deal with it differently though - the way she deals with it is to be super open about it. I don't really tell anyone but her about what happens at home, not properly anyway. But with these three - life, well - it somehow was bearable. We got through all the shit - if it was sat in the park drinking cans on a Saturday night or laughing at the back of Maths. We had each others backs and that was everything.

The girls are sat in a park. CHELSEA is smoking, JORDEN is eating Pick N Mix and HAYLEY is drinking a can of coke.

CHELSEA
Nah mate fuck her, she's a cunt.

HAYLEY
A dirty, saggy bell-end.

JORDEN
I weren't even on my phone.

KIRSTY
You were taking a selfie though girl.

JORDEN
Yeah but it weren't in view though.

KIRSTY
Well obviously you were you thick bitch. You got fake tan on your shirt.

JORDEN
Fuck off. Chelsea you got any fags left?

HAYLEY
Did you see what she was wearing today?

KIRSTY
Oh yeah; fucking Jesus shoes.

CHELSEA
What the fuck are Jesus shoes?

JORDEN
You know, those sandals that most people wear with socks.

KIRSTY
Or without socks to let their smelly, cheesy feet breathe.

CHELSEA
Ah mate, that's rank.

JORDEN
She's rank.

CHELSEA
Nah in all fairness she's a cunt but I'd still fuck her.

HAYLEY
You what?

CHELSEA
She's still quite fit.

KIRSTY
As far as miserable fucks go.

CHELSEA
I'd make her smile.

HAYLEY
Its probably closed up. No one would go near a dementer.

JORDEN
Chelsea, can I ask - I've always wondered actually -

KIRSTY
Oh here we go.

JORDEN
Nah mate, it's a genuine question.

CHELSEA
Well go on then.

JORDEN
Do you like - actually- you know?

CHELSEA
What?

JORDEN
Lick it?

CHELSEA
Uh...lick what?

JORDEN
The fanny.

CHELSEA
Well...um...do you suck cock?

HAYLEY
Mate, that's grim.

CHELSEA
True though innit?

KIRSTY
Yeah, well Hayley's never given head.

HAYLEY
Nothing wrong with that mate.

KIRSTY
Yeah, but just saying you can't really compare it to anything.

HAYLEY
That don't make me a lezzer. I still like guys and everything. I just don't want a cock in my mouth.

KIRSTY
Anyway it don't matter cos Chelsea's not licked a minge yet either.

CHELSEA
What the fuck are you? Virgin patrol?

KIRSTY
Nah, just saying; you might not like it.

CHELSEA
Do you reckon you won't like dick?

KIRSTY
I liked dick.

CHELSEA & HAYLEY
You sluuuuuut.

JORDEN
You hear that Venus is pregnant?

HAYLEY
Fuck mate. But then her sister had a baby last year. Makes sense don't it?

KIRSTY
I don't get why that should make sense? Surely if you're sister got pregnant at fifteen, you'd think to yourself - 'that ain't a good idea.'?

JORDEN
Your brother gay yet?

HAYLEY bursts into laughter.

HAYLEY
Yeah Kirst - you and Bradley can compare dicks you've sucked. Maybe you've sucked the sa-

KIRSTY
Fuck off, my brother ain't gay. He's nothing like the poof up in the flats.

CHELSEA
Only cos he knows your dad would fucking kill him.

KIRSTY
Fuck off would he.

HAYLEY
Mate, your dad is a proper bloke and so are all his mates. They'd slaughter him.

CHELSEA
I can just see him mouthing off down the Shipyard now.

PETER takes on the role of DAD and CASSIE takes on the role of STEVE. The band starts to play as we see them at the Shipyard pub.

DAD
So I go to fit a boiler the other day. I knock on the door and this black bird opens the door. You know- holding a couple of kids, hanging onto her like a tree. Fucking crying and wailing you know how they are, and I think to myself; oh, here we go.

STEVE
Too many foreigners.

DAD
Anyway, so I go inside and walk through the living room and see probably the bird's mum sat on the sofa, wearing what looks like these fucking pyjamas - you know that shit they wear, looking like they've got a fruit salad on their head and all that, and I try to find the boiler I say to her; "oi love, where's the boiler?" and she says, "It's just through here in the other room". Who the fuck she think she is talking down to me like I'm her fucking slave?

STEVE
Pint of Stella Artois.

DAD
I go into the kitchen - there's plates in the sink and kids toys on the floor. Fucking disgusting. Living like pigs mate.

STEVE
Nigel Farage.

DAD
And she offers me a cuppa. Like I'd want a cuppa made by her?

STEVE
Brexit.

DAD
So I start to fix the boiler, and the rude bitch just leaves the room. Leaves me to do my work. The fucking manners of it, and then when I'm finished she says; "oh great, just in time - I need to go to work."

STEVE
Stealing our jobs.

DAD
And then she pays me. I get back in the van and she drives away off to work presumably. I count the money. She's underpaid me. By 10p. Fucking foreigners.

STEVE
Get in Millwall.

DAD
Oh look, that fucking poof from the flats just walked in.

They mimic finishing their pints and the band stops playing. The focus shifts back to the girls.

KIRSTY
Suck your mum - my dad ain't racist.

HAYLEY
Oh come on, your dad definitely votes UKIP.

KIRSTY
Piss off - he doesn't.

CHELSEA
Aw-

KIRSTY
And also, my brother ain't gay.

JORDEN
Is.

KIRSTY
Isn't.

CHELSEA
Shit, I gotta go. Gotta baby sit Joe tonight. Mum's got a trial shift at a pub.

The girls get up and start to make tracks.

HAYLEY
Not the Shipyard is it Chels?

CHELSEA
Nahhh, it's the Furze Wren.

JORDEN
Bye.

The girls all say their goodbyes. CHELSEA and JORDEN exit. HAYLEY and KIRSTY hang behind.

HAYLEY
Mate, your snapchat was rough.

KIRSTY
Yeah and like that was filmed from just outside my bedroom. They were arguing in the kitchen.

HAYLEY
What'd she throw at him this time?

KIRSTY
A bottle of wine.

HAYLEY
Always fucking alcohol involved. My dad was mashed the other night - started getting lairey. Ended with me throwing Vodka in his face. Weren't so hard then.

The band starts playing. HAYLEY becomes MUM. The cast begin to dance, as if on a dance machine.

MUM
Where the fuck have you been?

DAD
Down the shipyard where I usually go on a Thursday night - and don't fucking swear at me.

MUM
BASTARD.

She throws something at him and the cast all jump, as if on a dance machine.

SINGER *Riffing*
Baaa-st-aaarrraaa—-rd.

DAD
Do you think I give a shit when you're not here on a Friday? It means I get some peace and quiet. You're fucking exhausting Julie.

MUM
Thing is, I'm actually at the pub and not with some whore.

DAD
You're paranoid. When the fuck do I have time to have some whore? I'm working all hours to support our family. You need to sort your head out love.

She slaps him. The cast act as if they are doing a forward motion on the dance machine.

SINGER *Riffing*
Stupid bii-yeaaaaahhh-itttch, ohhhhh yeah.

MUM
Do you think I enjoy looking after our kids day in, day out. I have to work as well you know - would help if you lifted a fucking finger - you bald bastard.

DAD
I'm surprised you're sober enough to know what day of the week it is love.

MUM
DIRTY OLD PERV.

She punches him in the stomach. The cast act as if they are doing a backward motion on the dance machine.

SINGER *Belting*
Dirty, old, PERRRRRRVV.

The next section of movement is faster and rhythmic. The cast go in various direction on the dance machine as MUM and DAD hurl various insults at each other. The singer goes wild vocally.

MUM
Cunt.

DAD
Slag.

MUM
Perv.

DAD
Shrivelled up prune.

MUM
Incompetent bastard.

DAD
Barren old whore.

She throws something at him; he ducks. The music and the cast stop.

DAD
It was fucking unnecessary to throw a chair at me Julie.

The cast and band begin to laugh uncontrollably, except KIRSTY. MUM and DAD go towards each other and hug, they begin to dance and laugh. The music starts and the cast begin to dance as well. The singer begins to improvise. KIRSTY sits down. MUM sees KIRSTY and the music stops.

MUM
Where you been?

KIRSTY
Just went out after school.

MUM
Where?

KIRSTY
Nowhere.

MUM
That's a weird sounding place, I ain't been there. Where is it?

KIRSTY
You're lucky you ain't been there.

MUM
Don't take the piss out of me Kirsty.

KIRSTY
I'm not. I'm gonna do my Drama coursework.

MUM
What, you gonna be an actress now?

KIRSTY
And so what if I wanna be?

MUM
Just saying, don't get your hopes up - how many people like us do you see in films? They're all posh pricks like Eddie Redbone and Keira Knightley.

KIRSTY
It's Eddie Redmayne.

MUM
Whatever.

KIRSTY
Alright - I'll just get a part-time job in a pub, get benefits and stay here for the rest of my life.

MUM
I'm not saying that. I'm just saying that, you've gotta be realistic in your expectations for the world. I wanted to be a Police officer when I was younger. I could have been as well.

KIRSTY
You chose to be the criminal instead.

MUM
That's the way you're heading - acting like a waster all the time.

KIRSTY
We've been studying this play in Drama. "A Taste of Honey" and the mum reminds me of you.

MUM
That sounds promising.

KIRSTY
She puts her daughter down all the time as well/ treats her like crap and then can't/ understand why her daughter don't like her.

MUM
What the fuck you talking about? I'm not/ putting you down or...listen/ I'm just being realistic. I understand why my daughter don't like me - she's going through her hormones and growing into a woman, I get that; I just don't want you to have your head in the clouds about this world. Get good GCSEs and then see if you can go to uni or get a good job.

KIRSTY
Yeah, I could go to uni like you. Oh, wait.

MUM
There you go again, getting spiteful. All three of you think you can talk to me the way you want - as if I don't have feelings.

KIRSTY begins to leave.

KIRSTY
I ain't got time for this.

MUM
Well I'll see you at dinner. Which I'm cooking - seeing as I'm such a horrible mother.

KIRSTY stops.

KIRSTY
Mum.

MUM
What?

KIRSTY
Did dad vote UKIP?

The band begins to play. JORDEN becomes NATHAN.

NATHAN
Ite babe.

KIRSTY
Hello.

NATHAN
You looked peng in English today, innit.

KIRSTY
Thanks.

NATHAN
You wanna come round mine and hang out? My parents ain't home, innit.

KIRSTY
No thanks.

NATHAN holds up a 'kiss emoji'.

KIRSTY is silent.

NATHAN
What you doing babe?

Silence.

I'm all on my own. I don't like feeling lonely, innit.

Silence.

Your eyes are stunning babe.

KIRSTY
Stop calling me babe; I don't even talk to you properly.

Silence.

NATHAN
Send me a piccy.

KIRSTY
What?

NATHAN
You know like a cheeky pic./ A naughty pic.

KIRSTY
No. Fuck off.

NATHAN
Ahhhhh April fools!

The band stops playing.

KIRSTY
It's January.

NATHAN exits and CHELSEA comes bounding in.

CHELSEA
You see that fucking stuck up new girl trying to sit with us today?

KIRSTY
Yeah, she's annoying, but -

CHELSEA
Fucking prances over with her long, blonde hair and her blazer done up, with her tie down to her knees like a fucking boffin.

KIRSTY
You didn't need to be so nasty to her though; she only asked if she could sit with us.

CHELSEA
Nah, fuck her - coming over to sit with us like she's one of us. She probably gets her fanny washed by her butler. What's she doing coming to this school anyway? "Look at me - my parents don't get benefits. I'm above you all."

KIRSTY
She probably ain't even rich; my parents only get a few benefits.

CHELSEA
Course she is. Look at her shoes - probably from Jimmy Choo costing three hundred quid. Cunt.

KIRSTY
You got any fags?

CHELSEA
Want one?

KIRSTY
Yeah. Fucking Nathan Godfrey was messaging me on Facebook last night.

CHELSEA
Getting a bit of sex eh?

KIRSTY
Fuck off. As if I'd touch that.

CHELSEA
Anyone who's got 'the 1 and only Natters Godfrey' as their Facebook name, wants stabbing.

KIRSTY
He thinks he's god's gift to girls.

CHELSEA
Oi, you know his brother gets proper cheap booze though?

KIRSTY
What's that got to do with anything?

CHELSEA
Just saying. Could come in handy for Ross Browne's party on Saturday.

KIRSTY
I ain't fucking Nathan Godfrey for cheap booze; there's more to life than cheap booze.

CHELSEA
I ain't saying you've gotta sleep with him, just send him some flirty messages.

CHELSEA
Nah, I ain't doing it, ain't worth it - and I ain't going to that party.

CHELSEA
Ah mate, you've gotta.

KIRSTY
Nah, he's a skank. Also, my dad's being really weird with me and Bradley at the moment. Says Saturdays are for us to bond as a family - he's trying to get mum settled.

CHELSEA
Bunk it off.

KIRSTY
It ain't school Chels. Anyway, I can't; it'd be nice if Mum would calm down.

CHELSEA
Doesn't mean you can't get us cheap booze.

CHELSEA grabs KIRSTY's phone.

KIRSTY
What the fuck/ you doing? Fucking give it back.

CHELSEA
I ain't gonna type anything too bad. Get off me. Ah don't matter - sent now.

The girls struggle over the phone. KIRSTY eventually gets it back.

KIRSTY
You little slag! He's gonna think he's in.

CHELSEA
You're just helping your mates out, that's all.

BRADLEY enters. He's looking for KIRSTY.

BRADLEY
There you are.

KIRSTY
What?

CHELSEA
Alright Brad?

BRADLEY
Alright. You get that text from mum?

KIRSTY
No, but I can guess.

BRADLEY
She's/ leaving dad.

KIRSTY
Leaving dad. What a surprise.

BRADLEY
Well, should-

KIRSTY
What do you want me to do about it?

BRADLEY
I dunno, but I feel like we should do something.

CHELSEA
Shit, I gotta go anyway. Gotta baby sit my brother - Mum's up the pub tonight.

KIRSTY
Oh, she get that job then?

CHELSEA
Nah....Talk to 'the 1 and only' please Kirst.

KIRSTY
Fuck off.

CHELSEA exits.
BRADLEY
Who's the one and only?

KIRSTY
Don't matter. Anyway - I don't see what we can do about it?

BRADLEY
I guess go and sort the situation.

KIRSTY
Dad and mum aren't gonna break up Brad. We'll go home; they'll be screaming at each other. Then one of them will hit the other, probably mum, and then they'll start throwing stuff at each other and then eventually they'll laugh about around breakfast tomorrow morning. There ain't nothing we can do.

We hear some voices shouting from across the park.

VOICES
Alright faggot? Gonna go suck some cock? Fucking queer.

KIRSTY looks at BRADLEY, who is deflated and she starts to leave.

KIRSTY
Come on then if you're coming.

The band start playing. KIRSTY and BRADLEY enter the house.

MUM
I'm going and there ain't nothing you can do to stop me.

DAD
Here we go - the same routine again. Here come the water works.

MUM
Yeah, you just laugh Ian. That's gonna change my mind you patronising bastard.

DAD
Ladies and gentleman - Meryl Streep.

MUM
You've laid your hands on me for the last time.

The band stops playing.

KIRSTY
And this is what Bradley's talking about. The same old routine. Mum and dad row over something trivial - the argument escalates; they get spiteful. Dad tries to end the argument and mum begins to get even more poisonous, bordering physical; start to hurt dad - until eventually he snaps and either hits her or pushes her to get her away from him. She starts to play the victim and threatens to leave - to try and get him to apologise. I've seen this all my life. *To BRADLEY* Brad, this is nothing to worry about.

The band starts playing.

DAD
Where you gonna go then, huh?
MUM
I'll go to a refuge for abused women - where you can't fucking find me.

DAD
Don't worry about me trying to find you.

MUM
Then you'll have to do all your own cooking, housework and clean the shitty skid marks out of your underwear yourself.

DAD
Probably do a better job, cos I won't be half cut all the time.

MUM
And I'll take the kids. Those fucking kids that I've had to deal with all on my own.

The band stops playing.

KIRSTY
Lovely. Thanks mum. And so we enter phase two. Mum threatens to take the kids - in a well rehearsed routine that has gone on for far too long and probably needs to change, because my brother Bradley, is just turning eighteen and I turn sixteen in June. Both of an age where we can decide on our own where we go.

The first time I remember mum planning to leave dad - I was young, like tiny. She came running into my room in the middle of the night, she looked fucking crazy; like Cruella DeVille in 'One Hundred and One Dalmatians'. You know the bit? When she crashes her car. She starts packing my clothes into a bag and I don't know what's going on. I start crying and I ask her to stop being scary. "Stop being scary mummy, please." She picks me up; everything's OK, cos mummy's got me. She's holding me tight and I feel safe. She runs into Brad's room, holding me, and rushes him out and we start to head down the stairs. As we go through the living room- all I can see is the back of dad's head. He sounds like he's crying. Mum pulls my face in close to her and I can hear dad saying; "Please Julie, stop this - your not thinking straight, you can't take my kids away. I'm sorry." He grabs me out of mum's arms and they're both struggling to hold onto me; I feel like a fucking rag doll. In the struggle - I hear Bradley start to scream and cry. I look up, and dad's face is covered in blood; his face looks like something from a nightmare. I start to scream, like scream the fucking house down - I'll never forget it. Dad starts crying too and says; "Calm down, it's only daddy. It's only me. I've just had a little accident, got a little cut on my forehead." Mum starts crying. We're all crying, and end up sat on the sofa. Sat crying together. Eventually we calm down and dad takes us back to bed. Whilst mum just sits there, not looking at us. Not looking at him. The next morning - everything was normal again. And I couldn't talk about it. I just wanted to scream at them - "What happened?! Why did that happen?". That's the worst it's even been. Phase two I mean. Although I think that maybe it's because I've become accustomed to it - this, this is just a way of life.

And now we move onto phase three, the final phase of the routine.

The band starts playing.

DAD
What you gonna do then Julie? Find some other mug to put up with your shit? Your aggressive behaviour and your lying? You're a sociopath.

MUM
You abuse me. I attack in self-defence.

DAD
Attacking first doesn't sound like self-defence to me.

MUM
Yeah, that's it - start on your mind games and trying to make me believe that I deserve it. That's how abusers like you work.

DAD
I know I ain't innocent. But you certainly ain't Snow bloody White in these fights.

MUM
You hurt me so much Ian - mentally and physically.

DAD
What about what you do to me? Physically and emotionally, fucking bullshit?

MUM
Oh yeah - that's it! I'M FUCKING CRAZY. I'm fucking mental. Why don't you just fucking leave me? WHY DON'T I GET A KNIFE AND JUST SLIT MY FUCKING WRISTS?!

KIRSTY
And with that, dad falls into the same trap as normal and he stupidly goes to comfort a hysterical mum. Rookie mistake - she slaps him and keeps going. He pushes her away with force.

MUM
Don't you fucking touch me.

KIRSTY
And with that she throws a photo frame at him.

The band begins to go wild.

DAD
Don't fucking throw things.

KIRSTY
Dad throws it back. She starts throwing anything she can find - the TV remote, ornaments, until after having half the living room thrown at him, dad restrains her and tries to calm her down.

The band stops playing.

End of phase three. It's over. Except...

The band starts playing. They gradually crescendo.

Dad restraining her hasn't worked. She bites him and in pain he lets go and she starts punching him. Like, no dainty slaps - fucking big Muhammad Ali type punches. Dad pushes her away, but she keeps going - she's fucking crazy - jumping on him; hitting him again and again. Dad hits her - to try and slow her down, but she doesn't stop. Bam - punch in the stomach. Dad falls down in pain wincing and she picks up a flower pot and starts hitting him. With, with - Bradley runs,over and he he tries; to - no Brad just leave it. He tries to pick her up, pull her away from dad but she's not stopping. Punching, hitting hard. Dad runs over to me at the door and mum throws the flower pot.

JUST STOP!

BRADLEY
Mum.

KIRSTY
I see the flower pot coming right at me.

The band stops playing. We hear a smash and KIRSTY falls to the floor.

HAYLEY enters.

HAYLEY
Mate that is one fucker of a shiner and your lip looks rough as.

KIRSTY stands up.

KIRSTY
Of course mum scrambled to help me up. Everything seemed to diffuse straight away. We've now established that all it takes is one of your kids to get in the way of one of your missiles and then everything calms down. Stand down soldiers. Dad's shouting at mum to tell her to leave me alone. I head up to my room. Shut them out. For fuck sake. The first time in my life I've ever been hit by my parents. And it's a fucking flower pot landing on my head.

HAYLEY
I always find the best thing to do in those situations is to get fucked as possible and then have it out with my dad.

KIRSTY
They were laughing about it all over a Weetabix this morning.

HAYLEY
Yeah mate - I can't say that ever happens in our house. We don't talk to each other for a couple of days and then everything calms down. We never laugh about it though.

KIRSTY
I think laughing is dad's coping mechanism. I don't think he really finds it funny. I can't take much more of it. It was worse last night. It went past phase three - you know what I mean?

HAYLEY
Shit's getting bad once another phase gets added on.

KIRSTY
No, but you don't understand; there ain't ever been another phase added on. It's always been the same way. But - last night; it was fucking disgusting.

HAYLEY
My dad got worse a couple of years ago for a while. We knew shit was bad when he got me confused for my mum and tried to fuck me.

They look at each other and burst into laughter.

KIRSTY
We're so fucked up.

JORDEN and CHELSEA enter and join HAYLEY and KIRSTY. CASSIE enters the other side of the stage.

JORDEN
What the fuck is she looking at?

CHELSEA
Maybe she fancies you?

JORDEN
Errrrr, you fucking lesbian. No offence Chels.

CASSIE
I wasn't staring at you.

HAYLEY
Well, look at the fucking board then and don't look at us.

CASSIE
Sorry.

HAYLEY
That didn't need an answer.

CHELSEA
Probably goes home and strums herself thinking about you Jorden.

JORDEN
That's grim.

CHELSEA
Probably dreams of licking you out.

JORDEN
What does it taste like?

CHELSEA
The fuck you chatting about?

JORDEN
Minge.

CHELSEA
I dunno. I've never tasted it.

JORDEN
I've always wondered what it tastes like. You know, when you squirt.

HAYLEY
For fuck sake.

CHELSEA
Fuck sake. I'm beginning to think you're a dyke as well.

JORDEN
No, I ain't. I just wondered, you know?

CHELSEA
You're that fucking interested, then go and taste your own next time you flick the bean.

KIRSTY
You two are so grim.

All this while - CASSIE has gradually begun to grow intrigued by the cut on KIRSTY's lip and black eye.

HAYLEY
What you wearing to Ross Browne's on Saturday? You sort that booze Kirst?

KIRSTY notices CASSIE.

KIRSTY
What you staring at?

CASSIE
I wasn't staring - I -

KIRSTY
Keep your eyes to yourself.

HAYLEY
Trying to get a glimpse of your face. Here, you know she got this when she got into a fight with a lad who tried to attack her on her way home last night. The lad came out worst.

CASSIE looks away.

CHELSEA
Nosey cunt.

The bell goes. The girls dissemble. CASSIE grabs KIRSTY as the others exit.

CASSIE
Sorry, could I - sorry, look; I mean -

KIRSTY
What do you want?

CASSIE
I'm sorry if it seemed like I was staring and being nosey - I just, look; the thing is. I just -

KIRSTY
Come on, spit it out.

CASSIE
What happened to your face?

KIRSTY looks at her. Stunned.

KIRSTY
You heard what happened. Hayley told you.

CASSIE
Yeah, but surely you'd need to go to the police?

KIRSTY
What's to say I ain't?

CASSIE
They didn't say anything in assembly earlier.

KIRSTY
What the fuck are you? Sherlock Holmes? I just don't want everybody knowing my business.

CASSIE
But surely for the safety of others -

KIRSTY
I don't know you. This is the first time I've fucking spoken to you and you think you can ask me personal questions like this?

CASSIE
I'm just saying, that maybe you should talk to -

KIRSTY grabs her.

KIRSTY
Fuck off posh girl. Keep your meddling to your Nancy Drewe books.

CASSIE exits.

KIRSTY
Saturday comes around, and being loyal to my mates; I arrange the booze from sending a few messages to Nathan Godfrey; saying that I'll maybe let him hang out with me after school if he sorts us out. I think to myself I might as well go to the party after all. The thing is, none of us are talking at home, after they laughed - no one said anything. Just pretending nothings happened. This time things went out of the comfort zone and into a dangerous, new territory. Me and Bradley ain't even talked about what happened. Saturday night comes around and I think to myself - fuck this. I'm gonna get mashed. After the chat I'm about to have with Bradley - I reckon I'm gonna need it.

BRADLEY enters.

BRADLEY
Kirst. Can I talk to you?

KIRSTY
What about?

BRADLEY
I dunno - well I do. I just, it's something I need to get off my chest.

KIRSTY
Yeah. Go on.

BRADLEY
I...I don't know how....I can't say it.

KIRSTY
What is it?

BRADLEY
I don't wanna say it.

They are in silence. BRADLEY struggles to find words.

KIRSTY
You get someone pregnant?

BRADLEY
No - it's worse than that, I just, I can't -

KIRSTY
You done drugs? Fuck sake Bradley - you're such a loser. What was it? A bit of weed? Everyone's done weed. I did weed when I was in year 9. You're so dram-

BRADLEY *Quietly*
I'm gay.

KIRSTY
What?

BRADLEY
I'm gay.

KIRSTY
What? No?

BRADLEY looks despondent.

I didn't mean it like that. I'm sorry, I didn't mean it like that. I just - I didn't expect you to say that. It's - oh shit. I'm sorry.

BRADLEY
Didn't you guess?

KIRSTY
I don't know. I like, I dunno - I guess maybe I thought you were, but like. I dunno - I thought maybe you were just like a bit sensitive.

BRADLEY
I've tried so hard to hide it though. This ain't exactly the rainbow capital of the world.

KIRSTY
It ain't like you're as gay as someone like, I dunno - like look at Chelsea. Now, she's making a proper statement about being gay. Cos of her haircut, Mrs Johnson's threatened to expel her five times.

BRADLEY
Everyone picks on me at school and I ain't even come out yet.

KIRSTY
It's just cos they think it might be your weakness. Look at your Brad; you're fucking gorgeous.

BRADLEY
You have to say that.

KIRSTY
No I don't. You're so much smarter than me, you've got a future - loads of people fancy you. The people who take the piss are just wasters who ain't gonna do anything with their life.

BRADLEY
You must think I'm a pervert.

KIRSTY
I thought you were anyway.

They laugh.

BRADLEY
I'm so scared. I don't wanna be gay.

KIRSTY
Why?

BRADLEY
Cos it's fucking weird. It's different. I wanna be like everyone else. Look at what happened to the poof up in the flats.

KIRSTY
Walking around here in tight pink shorts ain't exactly University Challenge intelligence is it Brad? Yeah people are a bit rough round here when it comes to being - you know? But, why would you wanna be like everyone else round here? You wanna get a girl pregnant and be trapped here for the rest of your life? You wanna end up wasting around and occasionally doing the odd robbery for a bit of extra cash? Have Belmarsh prison be your weekend home? Fuck 'em. You're you; and you're sound - you're gonna make something of yourself. That's all that matters. Who gives a shit if you like boys or girls - it don't change who you are.

BRADLEY
So, you don't think any different of me?

KIRSTY
Of course not. If anything I'm excited - you're my gay big bro. You've gotta start taking me to see musicals.

BRADLEY
Fuck that.

KIRSTY
You gonna tell mum and dad?

BRADLEY
I dunno. What if dad don't like it?

KIRSTY
Dad ain't a prick though - I dunno why people have ideas that he's a hard man. He'll still love you.

BRADLEY
Come on. Dad works in mechanics. He drinks at the Shipyard and he's got a Millwall tattoo. He's the embodiment of Thamesmead. He ain't gonna like it.

KIRSTY
Just cos dad seems like a bit of a stereotype don't mean he ain't capable of feelings.

BRADLEY
He probably votes UKIP.

KIRSTY suddenly hugs BRADLEY. They hug for a moment.

KIRSTY
I'm proud of you Bradley.

BRADLEY
You're hugging me. This -

KIRSTY
Nah it ain't right.

They break away from each other.

BRADLEY
Thanks Kirst.

The band start to play. Everyone enters and starts to dance.

HAYLEY
This party is fucking great!

CHELSEA
Nah mate, you can walk away right now.

JORDEN
Hi Kieran - I like your shirt.

PETER
Nah I don't want any weed thanks.

GERRY
Do you see how reem Peter looks tonight?

JAMES
I'm gonna throw up.

HAYLEY
You spill your drink on me again, I'll lay you out.

CHELSEA
Look at me - I'm a dyke. I ain't interested.

JORDEN
What's Kieran doing talking to Betsy Halton?

Between a Man and a Woman & F*ckingLifeMate. The Plays of Scott James.

PETER
Put on some Ed Sheeran.

MICHAEL
Anyone got any weed?

KIERAN
Betsy, you look so peng tonight.
The party disperses and begins to look more like a teenagers house party.

KIRSTY
Bog standard teenage house party. Stoners doing weed in the back garden. Drunk kids dancing in the living room and people getting drunk as fuck in the kitchen. Someone is being sick in both the downstairs and upstairs toilets and there's an argument going on at the top of the stairs, which means someone is definitely gonna fall down soon. The 'one and only Natters Godfrey' comes bounding over to me. Fuck, didn't realise he was actually gonna be here tonight.

NATHAN comes swaggering over to KIRSTY.

NATHAN
Alright Kirst.

KIRSTY
Alright.

NATHAN
You enjoying the booze my brother got?

KIRSTY
Yeah. One less WKD then we asked for though.

NATHAN
Alright, sorry. A thank you would be nice.

KIRSTY
Thanks.

NATHAN
Why don't you thank me in some other way?

KIRSTY
How? You want a written thank you card?

He moves closer to her.

NATHAN
Why don't we move upstairs?

KIRSTY
I'm fine just here thanks. I'm just waiting for the bog.

He moves his hand across her stomach.

NATHAN
Come on, don't be like that. I know you've been dying for this for a while.

KIRSTY
Oh, have I?

NATHAN
Wanna show me how you sucked Jack Ellis's cock?

He puts his hand on her breast.

KIRSTY
Get your hand off my tits now.

NATHAN
Ah don't be like that babe. My snake is bursting to get out.

She grabs him by the balls.

KIRSTY
Get the hell away from me or I'll fucking give you a real thank you and you won't fucking enjoy it you skanky cunt.

She lets go and he starts to move away.

NATHAN
You fucking little prick tease. Just using me to get cheap booze - slut.

KIRSTY
Let's be clear mate - that definitely ain't no snake - more like a worm. Cunt.

KIRSTY storms off and enters an empty bedroom. She enjoys being on her own for a moment.
Fucking prick.

She sits down and starts to enjoy being on her own.

JORDEN bursts in followed by CHELSEA. She is crying.

JORDEN
Who the fuck does she think she is? Fucking slagging it round the house all tonight. She knows I've fancied Kieran for ages. She's just fucking rubbing it in my face.

CHELSEA
You heard what Betsey Halton's done to Jorden?

KIRSTY
No, what's she done?

CHELSEA
She wants fucking doing - she really does. Fucking stood there in her Adidas hoody and Nike trainers. Fucking teenage chav. She's a pikey you know? She lives in the trailer park by Harrow Manor Way.

KIRSTY
What's she done?

JORDEN
Well, you know that like I was talking to Kieran for ages on Facebook right? Well, this week we got a little bit more serious. I gave him my number and we've been talking on WhatsApp.

CHELSEA
They even hung around together at lunchtime this week in the canteen, remember? On Tuesday?

KIRSTY
Ok, but what's happened?

JORDEN
So like, tonight we get here and Kieran's already here right?

CHELSEA
And Jorden goes over to him and says "Hi Kieran, I like your shirt."

JORDEN
I said "Hi Kieran, I like your shirt." And he just like says to me "You alright. You come with the girls?"

CHELSEA
And then he walks away. Like not paying attention to her.

JORDEN
I'm trying to get his attention all night and he's just not paying any attention to me at all. Just standing with the other lads, you know?

CHELSEA
And then right - I go outside about twenty minutes ago and I see him talking to Betsy. Oh, I'm gonna kick her.

KIRSTY
Wait, but what has Betsy done?

JORDEN
I'm gonna check her Instagram, I bet he's liked that slut's photos.

JORDEN frantically begins to check her phone.

CHELSEA
Don't you get it? She's fucking stolen Jorden's fucking man. Slutting it up all night so that Kieran'll pay attention to her and she can get her claws into him. She's always been jealous of Jorden.

KIRSTY
Wait, I'm confused - they were only talking. Also, Betsy and Jorden have like never spoken to each other.

CHELSEA
Have you lost your head? We need to do this slag, she's -

JORDEN lets out a guttural scream.

JORDEN
He's liked six of her photos. How could I be so fucking stupid?!

She sinks down in tears. It's as if she is dying.

CHELSEA
Babe, babe, babe - he ain't worth it. Neither of 'em are. He'll probably get her pregnant and she'll be fucked.

JORDEN
I wanted his babies.

HAYLEY bursts in.

HAYLEY
Mate, you guys wanna get downstairs. Nathan and Kieran just got into a fight cos he saw Betsy wanking Kieran off.

JORDEN dramatically springs to her feet and follows HAYLEY out, dragging CHELSEA with her.

JORDEN
Oh Kieran. That slag - I'll kill her.

After they have exited. KIRSTY exhales a big breath.

KIRSTY
Is it a bad thing to suddenly realise that all your mates are thick as shit? To have a realisation that you may be just wasting your time hanging around with them, and maybe I needed to get back on track and buckle down, cos I wanted to go somewhere. The thought was only fleeting, but it was a massive turning point without me even realising it. I sat there, on my own in this empty bedroom - with the door shut, just enjoying - enjoying the silence. Enjoying being on my own and not listening to the shit of my parents screaming at each other. The dull, irrelevant ramblings of the girls, crying about a boy not paying attention to them. Quite frankly, I'd never given a fuck about a boy paying attention to me. There was the time I'd had sex with Jack Ellis. We went out for about three weeks in year 9 and after about two weeks he begged me to suck his cock. I thought to myself - might as well. A couple of nights before - mum and dad had had this huge fight. It'd got to phase three and dad had restrained mum - well, I assume so anyway - I was up in my room so I could only sort of hear stuff. Anyway, after the fight - I heard mum and dad coming up the stairs. They were laughing, but their voices sounded different. Next thing I can hear mum and dad moaning. She's screaming "oh yes, yes, yes - fuck me, fuck me hard." They're banging the wall and I can hear the bed creaking. I put my pillow over my head and then try and put my headphones in, but I could still feel the wall slamming and vibrating. So, when Stephen begged me to suck his cock. I thought to myself. Why the fuck not? Those fuckers can have sex and make

it loud and fucking angry. So why can't I? And I took his cock in my hands and started to wank it, and then I started to suck it. And it's weird. All I thought of was them- and how they'd had sex a couple of days before. I didn't like it. It sort of made me feel sick. It's like, I almost did it to spite them, but couldn't get the image of my dad fucking my mum out of my head. Every time he groaned, all I could hear was mum's over the top, shrieky moans. Then he asked if he could fuck me. I thought to myself, well might as well - I'm already half way there anyway. So he put a condom on, I took his cock, and guided it up my skirt, moving my knickers to one side and let him push it in me. It fucking hurt. Next thing I knew, there was blood all over his cock, he didn't care he kept going; suddenly I could see why mum would moan the way she moaned when dad was fucking her. It fucking hurt. I was telling myself "Stop thinking of mum and dad." I thought I was gonna cry. Eventually he cum. He pulled out and it felt like someone had just put a slab of concrete up my fanny. We broke up the next week, so I didn't have to do it again. I didn't wanna do it again. I didn't get why all I'd thought of was my mum and dad having sex when I was having sex - surely that's not normal; it's kind of incestuous right? Anyway, I didn't have sex again after that. I didn't wanna have sex again after that. I was so worried that if I did it again, I would think about that night and visualise mum and dad again. Afraid that I might be fucked sexually cos when I'm having sex I thought about my parents. I didn't wanna put myself through that again. I didn't wanna risk it- until in walked Peter.

PETER enters. He is on the phone.

PETER
Yeah, yeah I know. Yeah I'm gonna stay at Toby's.

He notices KIRSTY

Oh, sorry. Look mum, I've gotta go. Yeah, yeah - OK, yeah me too.

He hangs up.

KIRSTY
You didn't have to hang up cos of me.

PETER
Bloody mums eh?

KIRSTY
Mate, my mum don't give a shit until I'm out of the house.

PETER
Mine's pretty needy. If I'm out, she'll ring me a couple of times to double check I'm OK.

KIRSTY
That's -

PETER
Sad?

KIRSTY
Nah, it's...pretty cute, pretty nice.

PETER
Until she's getting herself worried because you've moved from one place to another.

KIRSTY
You need one of them tracker things on your phone.

PETER
I don't want her knowing where I am twenty four seven. I'm not always where I tell her I am.

They laugh. KIRSTY looks at him for a moment. He lights a cigarette.
KIRSTY
Probably shouldn't smoke in here.

PETER
I don't think Ross is gonna do anything, he's too busy stopping the fight downstairs.

KIRSTY
I don't reckon his mum and dad will appreciate the smell of smoke all over their bed.

PETER
I'm Peter.

KIRSTY
Kirsty.

They look at each other for a moment. Awkwardly PETER breaks out of the silence.

PETER
You do music don't you?

KIRSTY
Yeah, how come?

PETER
I've seen you round the music block.

KIRSTY
Yeah, doing GCSE music. And drama - I think I wanna be an actress. You do music?

PETER
Yeah, I'm going into Year 12; so I'm starting to look at Music schools.

KIRSTY
What do you play?

PETER
Piano. You sing right?

KIRSTY
Yeah - how did you -

PETER
Could hear you singing through the door the other day as I went into the piano room.

KIRSTY
Oh fuck.

PETER
No, it was really good. You've got a really nice voice.

KIRSTY
It's for our composition module.

PETER
What's the song about?

KIRSTY
Well, it's about, this - this, girl; nah, it's stupid.

PETER
No go on. It's not.

KIRSTY
It's about...this girl; russian girl. Who works in this house, sort of like a maid I guess - whilst her masters fight all the time. Like literally physically fight all the time, and in the end she gets caught in the cross fire. And they kill her. See - it's stupid.

PETER
It's original.

KIRSTY
Yeah, well doing what everybody else does is shit innit?

PETER
Amen to that.

KIRSTY
You do drama as well?

PETER
GCSE; but I wanted to do Science A-Level and they clashed.

KIRSTY
We've been doing "A Taste of Honey" - did you do that one?
PETER
Nah, we did "Blood Brothers".

KIRSTY
It's sick. It's about this girl in the late fifties, who lives with her mum who puts her down all the time and don't give a shit about her- and so she meets this sailor, and he gets her pregnant, but then disappears. He's black and cos its the fifties it's a 'taboo'. The mum meets this new man and they fight all the time and tear strips out of each other. I can relate to the play a bit.

PETER
Why? Did a black man get you pregnant?

KIRSTY
Funny. Nah, the mum bit. Like, a mum who don't get you, and your parents tearing strips out of each other.

PETER
Sounds shit.

KIRSTY
Nah it's alright. You get used to it.

They sit looking at each other.

Sorry, mate - I don't know why I'm telling you all this. You just met me. It's way too much ha.

PETER
Nah, I don't mind. Can I hear your song?

KIRSTY
What?

PETER
I'd really like to hear your song again. If you don't mind, that is?

KIRSTY
I dunno. I don't normally sing in front of people. I just like - you know?

PETER
You don't have to if you don't want. I don't mind.

She looks at him. She starts to sing the song. PETER is entranced. As the song begins to climax; HAYLEY enters with CHELSEA and JORDEN. As HAYLEY talks the music all stops and everybody looks at her.

HAYLEY
What the fuck - you think you're Celine Dion?

The band begins to play and we get the idea that the party is over. Everyone parts ways. KIRSTY is walking home. PETER enters.

PETER
You shouldn't be walking home on your own.

KIRSTY
Why? Cos I'm a girl?

PETER
No, cos in Thamesmead you're likely to be stabbed. Anyone that is. Not cos you're a girl.

KIRSTY
Don't you worry about me. I can take care of myself. I should probably walk you home.

PETER
Yeah, don't worry - I definitely get that. I'd still feel better if I could walk you home?

KIRSTY
If you insist. Where do you live?

PETER
Bexleyheath.

KIRSTY
Alright posh boy.

PETER
It's not posh. They had to put plants in the water fountain cos people kept putting bubble mix into it.

KIRSTY
Oh golly gosh!

PETER
Piss off. You live round here?

KIRSTY
Yeah, bout a ten minute walk. Just past the park.

And we start walking. Everything else seems to just slip away. For the first time, well - feels like ever. I don't think about the shit at home, not worrying about my idiot friends. The greyness of Thamesmead seems to sink away into the night and everything...well - there's this feeling that I can't quite describe. Something feels different. It's calm. For the first time - it's fucking calm. He's soft. He talks properly; doesn't talk to me like I'm just a hole to fuck. He has bright, blue eyes and he looks clean. He sort of talks a bit like - I don't know; like I dunno; he sort of reminds me of Bradley, but like he's a bit more articulate. He seems sensitive; we talk about music and then we sit down at a bus stop by the park and the night just disappears. I look at my phone. We've been talking for an hour- it could have been, well - it felt like minutes.

KIRSTY turns to BRADLEY.

I better go.

PETER
Wish you didn't have to.

KIRSTY
Me too....bye then.

PETER
Yeah.

They stand in silence for a moment. They break into a kiss. The kiss gets more and more passionate. They stumble backwards. Music.

KIRSTY
And we were kissing, and we just didn't stop. Next thing I know, we're by a bush in the park. Kissing. I put my hand on his chest and instinctively feel my hand going down to his crotch. I feel that he's got a huge bulge.

PETER
Wait, wait. We don't have to do this. If you don't want to do this - we don't -

KIRSTY
I kissed him before he could finish talking. He started to put his hands up my shirt. *She puts her hand up her shirt.*

And next thing I knew, he'd undone my bra and was feeling up my tits.

She pulls her bra out.

He dropped it on the floor. He guided my hand to his shirt and I began to undo the buttons.

PETER
Oh my god, your boobs are amazing.

He undoes his shirt.

KIRSTY
Even though it was dark - I could sort of see that he was toned. I felt his body all over his stomach. I could feel something stirring up inside me and I just wanted to feel his skin against mine. I lowered myself down to the floor and pulled him on top of me. Kissing him, feeling his tongue in my mouth and touching mine. I could hardly contain myself. I felt his bulge. Rock. Hard.

He starts to undo his trousers and as he does it - whilst almost struggling for breath he says:

PETER
We don't have to do this - if you haven't done it before I mean. We can take it slow.

As he is saying this he undoes his trousers and starts to pull them down.

KIRSTY
I just pull down his boxers and next thing I know, I can feel my mouth round his cock. I wanted it so badly. I feel myself begin to gag and he grabs the back of my head. I keep wanking it.

PETER
Slow down, I think I'm gonna cum if you keep going like that.

She pulls down her knickers under her skirt.

KIRSTY
"Fuck me then", I said. And he went in. I was so wet, that it just slid in. I couldn't believe it. All I could think of was how much I wanted him. I didn't even know if he was enjoying it or not- but all I knew, was that I just needed him to bang me. He was inside me and something felt so beautiful about it. We were connected. We'd connected emotionally and now were connecting physically. Keep going, please just keep going.

PETER
Oh fuck, you're amazing.

KIRSTY
This. Is amazing.

PETER
I'm gonna cum.

Both move as if they have orgasmed. Music stops.

KIRSTY
I felt it going inside me. Warm, soft. He kept sort of - I don't know, like shaking, shuddering as it sped inside me. Eventually, it slowed down. We looked at each other. He kisses me. And we start to get up, finding our clothes. He does his shirt up and pulls up his boxers and trousers. I put my knickers back on and put my bra into my bag. He walks me home and we say goodbye. I take his number. We kiss. I walk up the stairs to my bedroom. I get into bed. I start to fall asleep; and I suddenly realise. I didn't think of mum and dad having sex. Yes! Get in. I'm not a fucking perv.

CASSIE enters.

CASSIE
Kirsty, please, look - can you just stop for a minute.

KIRSTY
I don't know where this quote comes from, but I heard it Bridget Jones - "It's a truth universally acknowledged that when one thing in your life begins to go well, the rest comes crashing down". Or something like that. Monday morning - I get told by Boardy baby, (our form tutor) that I need to go and see Miss Lockley. The school councillor. What the fuck? Boardy announces it in front of the class so everybody watches me walk across the room to the door, looking at me like I'm a fucking fruit cake. I see that posh bitch Cassie sat in the corner - looking guilty as fuck. I make eye contact with her, and I know. I know - that bitch has gone and spoken to someone about me. Like it's her fucking business. I walk down to Lockley's office. My heart's beating, racing. What if I have to talk about everything that happened with mum and dad when they went further than phase three?Would they have called home? Would they have spoken to Brad? Shit - gotta come up with a story and fast. I can't use the one that Hayley came up with, cos then I'll have to talk to the police; they won't let an attack go unreported. Shit, fucking cunting shit. I could kill that bitch. I knock on the door. I swallow, it feels like I've swallowed my brain, what the fuck do I say- what the fuck. She's opened the door and tells me to go in and sit down. WHAT THE -

Music. CHELSEA becomes MISS LOCKLEY.

MISS LOCKLEY
Now this is nothing to worry about Kirsty. This is just something that I have to do when someone raises a concern to me. It's nothing formal, I just wanted to have a quick chat with you.

KIRSTY
Alright.

MISS LOCKLEY
Someone came to me on Friday and said they'd seen you with a black eye and a cut on your lip. Is that true?

KIRSTY
I...yeah.

MISS LOCKLEY
Do you mind telling me how that happened?

KIRSTY
I felt my heart stop. What the fuck do I say? She's looking at me. Fucking looking at me with those squinty, knowing eyes. Think Kirst. Think - think! THIIIIINNNK! And then it came to me.

To MISS LOCKLEY

I got into a fight with my cousin.

MISS LOCKLEY
With your cousin?

KIRSTY
Yeah, this stupid fight over a boy.

MISS LOCKLEY
How old is your cousin Kirsty?

KIRSTY
Fourteen.

MISS LOCKLEY
And you got into a fight over a boy?

KIRSTY
That's what I said innit?

MISS LOCKLEY
Is your cousin a student here?

KIRSTY
Nah, she goes Erith.

MISS LOCKLEY
So, it was just a little squabble with your cousin over a boy?

KIRSTY
Yeah, I just said that. It's nothing big.

MISS LOCKLEY looks at her for a moment.

MISS LOCKLEY
Well, might I suggest that next time you're a bit more careful when it comes to dealing with issues like that. Maybe avoid getting physical.

KIRSTY
Yeah, right.

Music stops.

Phew, covered that one. Only fucking just - Lockley ain't stupid. I'll kill that nosey cunt. Lunchtime with the girls.

CHELSEA, HAYLEY and JORDEN are sat at lunch.

CHELSEA
Did Lockley wanna see you about your face?

JORDEN
Why don't she mind her own business?

CHELSEA
What did actually happen to your face Kirst?

KIRSTY
I -

HAYLEY
As long as you didn't tell her that your mum threw a plant pot straight at your face.

KIRSTY looks at HAYLEY stunned.

CHELSEA
Fuck off. Your mum fucking through a plant pot at you?

KIRSTY
Yeah, but it's not as it sounds.

JORDEN
Why would she do that?

HAYLEY
Her parents are fucking mental. Throwing shit at each other all the fucking time. Hitting each other; proper tearing strips off each other. Makes me feel fucking good about my family. They're basket cases. Kirst, was just lucky enough to get caught in the middle.

CHELSEA
Fucking hell.

KIRSTY
It ain't like that.

JORDEN
Why didn't you tell us Kirst?

HAYLEY
She didn't think you guys would get it. No big deal.

CHELSEA
It fucking is. Don't you trust us.

KIRSTY
Nah, it's not that. I - I only told Hayley cos, you know - she like-

CHELSEA
Yeah I know her dad is fucking mental too, but that don't mean that we wouldn't understand. Any other secrets you're fucking keeping from us?

KIRSTY
And then, suddenly, out of nowhere - I started to cry. Hayley went to hug me and I snapped.

HAYLEY goes to hug KIRSTY.

Fuck you. Who the fuck do you think you are telling people about my life?

HAYLEY
Oi, I ain't the one that told Lockley am I?

KIRSTY
I walked away from them; quickly trying to find somewhere that I could just sit and die. I don't know if I'd ever been so embarrassed.

JORDEN
Oh Chels - I tried it you know.

CHELSEA
Tried what.

JORDEN
My own jizz - it's kind of sweet.

KIRSTY
I found myself sat behind the sixth form block. No one ever went there. Unless they were going to smoke or get off with someone. And even then they didn't pay any attention to anyone else.

CASSIE enters.

CASSIE
Kirsty, I -

KIRSTY
Fuck off. Who do you think you fucking are? This is none of your business.

CASSIE
I know, but I was worried. When I saw your face, it just...look I -

KIRSTY
You have no right to be worried. Who are you - Mother Teresa?

CASSIE stands in silence whilst KIRSTY cries.

CASSIE
I just worried you might be going through the same thing.

KIRSTY
The fuck you talking about?

CASSIE
I didn't want you to be going through the same thing as me.

KIRSTY
What?

CASSIE takes a deep breath. She sits down next to KIRSTY.

CASSIE
You know I only came to this school a few months ago? Well - I used to go to Farringtons in Chislehurst. You know - the private -

KIRSTY
I know what Farringtons is. I ain't thick.

CASSIE
I don't think you are...Well anyway, I was at Farringtons, and umm my dad was an investment banker. Mum - works in charity. Dad lost a really big job, and, he started drinking. A lot. He'd be out all hours and then when he came home - he'd be really drunk. Stinking of booze. He came home one night whilst we were eating dinner and he smelt so bad of alcohol that it made me feel sick. Half the time he couldn't see straight. Mum and dad went into a really rough patch and they started arguing all the time. My dad was using language that I'd never heard him use before. It was crazy - he was a total different person. He couldn't admit that he had a problem and things just got worse and worse. I came home from school one night and mum looked awful. Her face was all red and swollen. Her eye was almost closed up. I asked her what was wrong and she wouldn't talk to me. She just turned away and told me to go to my room. I went up to my room and hours later I could hear mum shouting, and then dad screaming. It was so loud and I just wanted to bellow at the top of my lungs - "Just stop it! STOP IT!" Eventually I couldn't stand it anymore and I did - I ran down the stairs and screamed at them to stop. As I walked into the room - dad was on top of mum; he was beating her. Hitting her so hard and she was just crying and screaming and I couldn't stop it. I kept screaming for him to stop but it wasn't working. So I grabbed him. I grabbed his face and pulled it, hoping that he would stop, but he just turned around...and he...

She has choked up. She wipes a tear away.

KIRSTY
How did you end up coming here then?

CASSIE
We lost our house. Dad lost all our money; drinking, gambling, spending it all. We had to move around here and I was put into this school...I didn't want to meddle in your life, but I - when I saw your face, it brought back all of those feelings. All of the fear, the disgust - the shame; and now, we're stuck on the estate. And I just wanted to stop someone from going through the same thing as me. I'm sorry.

KIRSTY
Does it still happen?

CASSIE
They go to marriage counselling. But there are times where it still gets fraught.

KIRSTY
It's fucking shit ain't it?

CASSIE
I thought - if I could stop someone else going through it; then, maybe it would make it easier for me to cope with what happened in my home and what had happened to me.

KIRSTY
Has it?

CASSIE
Now I just feel awful about home and the fact that I've made things bad for you.

They sit in silence for a while. KIRSTY breaks the silence.

KIRSTY
It's alright. I guess...you were just trying to help.

CASSIE
That's why I was staring.

KIRSTY
Yeah, I guessed that.

And then, I dunno - I just opened up to her. Started telling her about everything; the phases, the noises, what had happened when I was fourteen when I heard them shagging through the wall. I told her all about the first time the phase routines started. And- she - just listened. It weren't like Hayley- who always comes in with "yeah it's like what happens with my dad"; where she pretends to give a shit but really just wants to talk about her shit. Cassie was...actually listening. She just sat there, and listened to everything.

The bell rings.

Cassie - I don't suppose you want to hang out at some point; like at the weekend, or after school at some point?

CASSIE
I'd really love that.

KIRSTY
We went back into form and as we walked in - I saw the girls sat at the back. I went to walk over to them; but I thought - nah fuck 'em. Making my home life about them. Hayley sharing all my fucking business.

KIRSTY sits next to CASSIE.

HAYLEY
You fucking serious?

CHELSEA
She's that desperate to make a point that she goes and sits next to Beatrice Potter.

JORDEN
Who the fuck is that?

CASSIE *Whispered to KIRSTY*
It's actually Beatrix Potter.

KIRSTY
I barely spoke to the girls for ages after that. Like we'd say hello every now and then - occasionally talking on Facebook. Chelsea would sometimes message me, just to check that everything was OK. I appreciated that. But the more I spent time with Cassie - I realised that I actually had nothing in common with those girls. The only thing we had in common was that we had shit homes and went off the rails together; maybe Hayley sharing my shit did me a favour? I reckon it may have opened my eyes. I wanted good GCSEs; I actually did wanna do well. I wanted to be an actress or a drama teacher, or - something. I wanted to do something; I wanted to get out of the shitty prison that is Thamesmead. The estate. Those girls just wanted to smoke and drink and doss around. None of 'em gave a shit if they left school with no GCSEs and ended up in the same position as their parents. In a council house, with no prospects and the only concern was when the next dole payment was coming so that they could get fags and booze. Me

and Cassie - I mean, we actually did stuff. Like, we went and had coffee; I'd never had coffee before - but I found out that I quite liked Almond Lattes. We went to book shops and as a present; she bought me a play she thought I'd like - "All My Sons" by Arthur Miller and then we went to the theatre. We went to the fucking theatre. There was somewhere near us that was doing "A Taste of Honey" and she insisted that we went. We got all dressed up and went and watched it. It's really embarrassing, but I cried. Seeing the play that I'd read about twenty times on stage in front of me - it was so overwhelming; I felt like I could be Jo; I felt like I was there with her. I'd never been to a play before. Even though Cassie was different from me; we really understood each other. And she made me want to be a better person. She didn't really swear much - she didn't smoke, she didn't wanna go out and get wasted at the weekend. She wanted to do stuff; she wanted us to study together so we could both do well. She actually cared about me. I had someone who gave a shit about me.

CASSIE texts KIRSTY.

CASSIE
Did you want to go the cinema after school tonight? We could go and see that film with Colin Farrell and Nicole Kidman?

JORDEN texts KIRSTY.

JORDEN
Hey babe, hope you're ok. We miss you. Just wondered if you wanted to come with us today? We're bunking and gonna go up London. Meet us at Woolwich DLR at eight if you're coming.

KIRSTY looks at the two of them.

KIRSTY
Yeah sounds great. What time you getting to school Cassie? Wanna meet by the bakery to get a coffee before we go in?

BRADLEY enters.

BRADLEY
Kirst. I did it. I told him.

KIRSTY
Dad?

BRADLEY
Yeah - I can't believe it.

KIRSTY
How did he take it?

BRADLEY
I followed him into the shed where he was getting his tools.

DAD enters. BRADLEY walks up to DAD.

Dad - I need to talk to you about something if you've got time?

DAD
Not got that long, but what's up?

BRADLEY
I've got something to tell you; but you gotta promise not to get angry.

DAD
What is it? You broken something?

BRADLEY
Nah it's not that - well...I -

DAD
You in trouble at school?

BRADLEY
No, I -

DAD
With the Police? Anyone bullying you - we can get it sorted -

BRADLEY
Dad, I'm gay.

Music.

I felt the floor escape from underneath me. I wanted to fucking die. I saw his face taking it in. His expression changed. My mind began to race.

DAD
You fucking kidding me? You telling me that you're a fucking bender? A shirt lifter? Nah this ain't happening. I can't have my boy be queer. This ain't right. You ain't right. You're sick. You're no son of mine. The poof from the flats is a fag - not you. You can't be. Nah - I can't take this. I'll fucking kill you.

He begins to get aggressive.

Here Steve, my fucking so called 'son' is queer. Come and help me sort him out. You homo. Faggot. Bender. Gay boy. I'll kill you - I'll beat it out of you.

Music stops.

BRADLEY
He didn't say all that though. He just said.

DAD
That ain't news to me son.

BRADLEY
What?

DAD
I know you're gay.

BRADLEY
How do you know?

DAD
I picked up on the signs a long time ago.

BRADLEY
What signs?

DAD
You ain't ever been interested in girls for a start.

BRADLEY
I tried to be.

DAD
Yeah, but I could tell you were trying to be. And then you're best mate Kylah fancied you and anyone could see she was desperate for you to ask her out. She's fucking beautiful and you didn't even blink an eye.

BRADLEY
I'm sorry.

DAD
I don't fucking care mate. It's not like you chose to be gay.

BRADLEY
You don't mind?

DAD
The only thing I mind - is that people can still be nasty. I don't want people to target you cos you're gay. I mean look at the poof...shit sorry/ - gay guy in the flats. He gets shit all the time.

BRADLEY
It's fine. Yeah, but in all fairness; he does flaunt it around and make a statement.

DAD
True - that's probably a defence mechanism though. You don't need a defence mechanism though; cos you've got me. There ain't nothing wrong with how you are boy. But you've gotta promise that if you're gay - you're still gonna bring your good looking mates round.

BRADLEY
I'll try.

DAD
Come here.

DAD pulls BRADLEY in for a hug.

I'm proud of you, and your sister - whatever you are. I know me and your mum have our problems. But I love you two more than anything in the world.

KIRSTY punches BRADLEY.

KIRSTY
See, you nob end. I told you dad would be cool - and I'm telling you, he probably voted Labour.

BRADLEY
I'm gonna tell mum.

KIRSTY
When?

BRADLEY
I dunno.

KIRSTY
You want me to be with you?

BRADLEY
That'd be nice.

BRADLEY exits.

KIRSTY
But whilst I was finally beginning to get my head down and also enjoy spending time with someone who was a good influence on me. There was this new, fucking terrifying worry in the back of my mind. I was late. I hadn't had my period. I hadn't had it for about eight weeks. Since me and Peter had sex in the park. We hadn't used protection and like the fucking stupid bitch I am - I'd thought nothing of it. With what was going on at home and with everything else - it had just become something that completely left my mind. It was fucking shit, because things had calmed down. After what had happened with the flower pot - mum and dad were on their best behaviour. Bradley was finally facing up to who he was and I was in a much more settled friendship than the group I had been in. My GCSE predictions had come back pretty good; maybe I could stay on at sixth form and be a smarty pants like Brad. I was getting weird cravings. Olives and lemon slices - I didn't even fucking like Olives. I knew something was wrong.

CASSIE
I like the dress she's wearing in this.

KIRSTY
Cassie, I think I'm pregnant.

Silence.

CASSIE
What?

KIRSTY
I'm late. And I'm getting cravings.

CASSIE
Fucking hell!

KIRSTY
That's the first time I've heard you sw-

CASSIE
That came out of nowhere.

KIRSTY
I've been worried about it for about a week now.

CASSIE
Crap. What are you gonna do?

KIRSTY
I dunno. I'm fucking terrified. My mum'll kill me. My dad'll kill him.

CASSIE
Is it -

KIRSTY
Peter's? Yeah.

CASSIE
Are you gonna tell him?

KIRSTY
I haven't spoken to him for about a month, and you know - it just kind of fizzled out after that night. He just pretends I don't really exist every time I've seen him since that night.

CASSIE
You've got to do a pregnancy test.

KIRSTY
I know.

CASSIE
If you come to mine after school we can do one.

KIRSTY
I'm scared.

CASSIE
You're gonna have to do it. This won't go away.

CASSIE takes KIRSTY's hand.

We'll get this sorted. We'll get the test after school, yeah?

KIRSTY
And so the next thing I know - we've finished school and we're in the chemist. I'm looking at the pregnancy tests. There are so many of them - they all just look like a blur. I think I'm gonna pass out. I think I'm gonna cry. I think I'm gonna be sick. Cassie picks one up.

CASSIE
I'll get this one.

CHELSEA has noticed the girls. She speedily moves over to them.

CHELSEA
Fucking hell.

KIRSTY
Shit.

CHELSEA
Is this yours?
CASSIE
Yeah, but don't say anything.

CHELSEA
Shit. What you gonna do Kirst?

KIRSTY
I don't fucking know do I? I'm gonna do the test, I guess.

CHELSEA
Come back to mine - there ain't no one there and we can get this sorted.

KIRSTY
Nah - you're alright.

CHELSEA
Look - I know we've been fucking shit. We let you down. I know that. I feel fucking awful cos of it. Please, just let me help you out now.

CASSIE nudges KIRSTY.

CASSIE
Come on, she wants to help.

KIRSTY
We ended up at Chelsea's house. I pissed on the stick. I was shaking. It was the longest three minutes of my life. I've never been so scared. I felt paralysed. What the fuck was I gonna do if I was pregnant? What could I offer a fucking baby - I was a kid mys-

CASSIE
How long is left on it?

CHELSEA
Got another minute. Look I'm gonna make it easy for ya babe. If you're not pregnant I'm gonna say 'you're safe'. If you're pregnant - I'm gonna say 'Your life is gonna change.'

They are in silence until the phone pings. CHELSEA looks at the test. KIRSTY looks like she's going to pass out.

Babe - I'm so, so, sorry.

KIRSTY
What? Am I?

CASSIE
Fuck.

CHELSEA passes KIRSTY the test. She looks at it for a good while.

CASSIE
You OK?

CHELSEA
Course she ain't alright.

CASSIE
Oh, yeah - sorry.

KIRSTY walks over to the other side of the stage. She sits down. They are silent.

CHELSEA
I'm all for giving her time, but she's been in that bathroom for nearly an hour now.

CASSIE
Maybe we should try and get her out?

CHELSEA
Kirst. Come out - come on we can sort this.

CASSIE
Come out and we can sort out what we're gonna do.

CHELSEA
You sound weird when you say 'gonna'.

CASSIE
What? What do you mean?

CHELSEA begins to laugh.

CHELSEA
Nah it's weird, you just sound really posh. You sound funny when you swear as well.

CASSIE
What, like when I say 'fuck'?

CHELSEA laughs more and so does CASSIE.

CHELSEA
Mate that's fucking amazing - say shit.

CASSIE
Shit.

CHELSEA
Minge.

CASSIE
Minge.

Both are laughing uncontrollably.

CUNT!

As she says this KIRSTY opens the door. Both try and stop laughing.

KIRSTY
I'm gonna have to talk to Peter.

CASSIE
What are you gonna say?

KIRSTY
I'm just gonna tell him that I'm pregnant.

CHELSEA
Want one of us to come with you?

KIRSTY
No. Probably go down better if I tell him on my own. I'm meeting him in twenty minutes.

I went to meet him. It's funny. I felt numb. The waiting to find out was worse than the actual realisation that I was pregnant. As I walked to meet him. I looked at the blossom beginning to appear on the trees. Felt slightly poetic really - new life forming on the trees; whilst there was a life forming inside of me. Peter was already waiting by the park. I looked at him and all I could think of was that night. That perfect night. That perfect night that had created this fucking shit situation.

PETER
You alright?

KIRSTY
I need to talk to you about something.

PETER
What is it?

KIRSTY
I think you know.

He looks at her. Trying to work it out. It hits him suddenly.

PETER
You're not?

KIRSTY
Yeah.

PETER
I thought you were on the pill.

KIRSTY
No.

PETER
What, so you let me have sex with you, even though you knew that you weren't protected.

KIRSTY
It's not like that. It's -

PETER
Well what is it like?

KIRSTY
There was so much shit going on, that I just didn't think about what was going on and I -

PETER
Fuck. Fuck. Fuck.

KIRSTY
I just wanted to tell you.

PETER
I'm going to fucking music school. What the fuck?

KIRSTY
Well I didn't plan on this either.

PETER
Well it's not like you've got as much to lose as me.

KIRSTY
Are you kidding me?

PETER
What, you trying to get your benefits before you leave school?

KIRSTY
Oh fuck this.

PETER
How do you know it's even mine?

KIRSTY
Because you're the only person I've had fucking sex with.

PETER
So you're trying to trap me then?

KIRSTY
It ain't about that. I came to ask you what you think we should do?

PETER
Fuck this. Fuck this. Fuck you.

KIRSTY
I can't believe this.

PETER
You can't believe this?

KIRSTY
I literally just found out that I was pregnant, and I thought it was the decent thing to fucking tell you. You know what? Forget it. I'll deal with it on my own.

She begins to leave.

PETER
Wait. Wait - wait. What are you gonna do?

KIRSTY
Do you think that I want this? Do you think I wanna be tied down to a baby just after I've turned sixteen? I'll be sitting my GCSEs when I'm just beginning to show. Can you imagine having to collect your GCSE results when you're six months pregnant? Knowing that everyone's gonna be staring at you? 'Hey look - it's her, that Kirsty Bosworth who got pregnant before she was sixteen. She'll probably go on the dole when the baby's born and then settle down in a council house. You know her mum had her when she was eighteen?' Do you think that you'll have to live with that? People looking at you with disgust. Like you need to be ashamed. Nah, you'll be able to fuck off to music school and forget that this ever happened if you wanted to. When I have this baby - it's gonna be born into a house in which my mum and dad tear strips off of each other all the time. Where it's mum has had fucking things thrown at her head trying to get in-between the two of them. Imagine - all your hopes, all your dreams to move away from this hell-hole and make a good life for yourself; have a degree, have a career disappear from the moment you see two lines appear on a fucking stick.

She begins to cry.

I mean, fucking look at me. Like mother, like daughter. Pregnant when she's still in her teens - but hey, at least I've beaten my mum's record. This place really traps you doesn't it? You end up fucking stuck here; no future. No fucking life. Only nappies and single mum allowance. Well done me - I'm just another fucking figure in the Daily Mail on statistics of teenage pregnancies.

PETER has began trying to comfort her and he pulls her close whilst she cries into him.

He held me. He held me - and it felt so familiar; so safe. Just like that night. That night that had changed everything. What the fuck was I gonna do. I weren't ready to be a mother and from his reaction - he certainly weren't ready to be a dad. Me and him talked it through - and he said he'd try and be there; no many what happened. Cassie let me stay at her's that night and I laid there - on a mattress on the floor; with it all running through my head again and again. There was only one thing I could do. Well, only one thing that seemed right for me.

CASSIE appears.

CASSIE
Are you sure you want to go through with this?

KIRSTY
We stood outside the clinic and I looked at the door. A painted blue door. It looked proper posh. Like something from 'Oliver Twist' or something. Cassie had booked a private appointment with some of her savings for me at this place in Brixton.

CASSIE
Apparently it's over really quickly.

KIRSTY
I've gotta do this. It's the right thing to do.

As we entered the clinic and sat in the waiting room - I could see all these other women. I knew that they were all there for the same thing as me. Because they wanted to get rid of their babies. It made me feel sick and the weird thing is - I found myself judging them; almost beginning to think to myself "My situation is different." But then I thought - maybe it's not, maybe I'm just as bad as them. I had to stop thinking like this; it was the right thing to do; and there weren't anything wrong with what the other girls were doing. It wasn't a baby yet, and it wouldn't be fair to have this baby...but maybe I could have the baby and get it adopted? But how could I do that; just hand a baby over to someone else- a baby that I'd carried. STOP. Stop thinking like this - it's the right thing to do. You need to stop this.

CHELSEA becomes the NURSE.

NURSE
Kirsty Bosworth?

KIRSTY
Shit - fuck, no I don't know if I'm ready yet. You've gotta do this Kirsty. You have to.

KIRSTY walks towards the NURSE and she sits her down in a chair.

She talks me through all the precautions and potential side-effects of the abortion and double checks that I wanna go through with it. I tell her that I want to go through with it. She gets these two pills out.

NURSE
These two pills will terminate the pregnancy. You need to take the first one with a glass of water.

KIRSTY
I look at Cassie, and then I put the tablet in my mouth and take the drink of water.

She needs to put the second one in my vagina. She puts on her gloves and puts the tablet in there. I can just feel it there. I know what's about to come. This is it. It's gonna be gone.

They are on the train.

CASSIE
You OK?

KIRSTY
I'm fine.

She doubles over in pain.

I could feel it. These heavy pains. Like the worst period you could ever have. The baby inside me was dying. It was going away. That was it. I wasn't pregnant anymore, or very soon I wouldn't be. In the space of less than twenty four hours I'd gone from sitting in Chelsea's bedroom - waiting for the test to sat on the train, in agony because two tablets were killing it. It's like nature's way of punishing you for fighting it. I swear I could feel it moving around - I could feel my insides destroying it. Any trace of a pregnancy would be gone. Done. Life would be simple if your head could do what your body did. Erase any trace of something - erase the thought that I had done this.

BRADLEY enters.

Shit. Shit. Fuck. Shit. Brad. I told fucking Bradley I'd help him tell mum. I get off the train back to Abbey Wood and in pain - I walk as fast as I can to get home - I need to put what's just happened to the back of my head; I've gotta be there for Bradley. I walk in the front door and Bradley is sat down with mum in the living room.

BRADLEY is sat with MUM.

BRADLEY
And I just wanna get it off my chest. Because I hate feeling like I'm keeping a secret from you.

MUM
What is it? You get someone pregnant?

BRADLEY
I spoke to dad about it and he's alright with it -

MUM
Well, if your dad's alright about it - it can't be that bad.

KIRSTY enters. She is holding her stomach.

And where the fuck have you been? I was trying to call you last night.

KIRSTY
Sorry - I stayed at Cassie's.

MUM
And you didn't think to let me know? I was worried. The only reason I knew you were OK is cos I saw you were active on Facebook. What's the matter with you?

KIRSTY
I'm fine - just got bad period pains. It's fine.

MUM
I don't know what's worst - your chavvy mates or your knew posh mate who makes you think you're better than everyone else.

KIRSTY
Cassie ain't a snob.

MUM
She makes you think you're fucking Einstein.

BRADLEY
Mum - can I carry on with what I was saying?

MUM
Yeah, sorry Bradley. Go on - go and do some Drama play reading or something, I've gotta talk to your brother.

BRADLEY
Actually - I think I'd like it if Kirsty stayed. I've spoken to her about it already.

MUM
Fucking hell - so I'm the last one to know as usual. What is it?

There's a slight pause. KIRSTY goes to BRADLEY and holds his hand.

BRADLEY
I'm gay.

MUM sits in silence for a moment.

MUM
What?

BRADLEY
I'm gay.

MUM
Are you joking? What the fuck? No you're not.

BRADLEY
I am. I'm gay.

MUM
No. No - I can't believe you'd do this. And why would you tell your dad before me?

BRADLEY
It's not about dad. I wanted to get it off my chest and tell you both, but -

MUM
But you'd rather tell your dad first?

BRADLEY
No, it's not that. Mum it's nothing to do with -

MUM
Fucking typical of this family. Crazy mum isn't told anything - everything's kept from Mum. I can't deal with this.

She goes to walk out. KIRSTY follows her. Something snaps inside her.

KIRSTY
Hang on - this isn't fucking fair. Bradley's just told you something that he's been coming to terms with for years and then you just disregard it as if you've been wronged.

MUM
You keep out of this Little Miss Self-Righteous. Now that you've got your posh mate you think you know everything about anything.

KIRSTY
Mum, you're making this all about you. This isn't about you. It isn't about dad. It's about Bradley.

MUM
I'm not making it all about me; I'm just sick of not being told anything. You're all selfish.

BRADLEY
I didn't tell you first because I knew you'd react like this.

KIRSTY
You only understand your own problems. You don't get that we all have shit going on mum.

MUM
You could have told me anything. You're my son - I'd listen to anything. Everything. I can't believe you'd fucking do this to me. Go on, tell me. Fucking tell me. You think you can tell your dad? Tell me - tell me everything. Who you with then? Who you been sneaking around with? Come on fucking tell me!

BRADLEY
Alright. You wanna fucking hear everything? Seeing as I'm out to hurt you - why don't I fucking tell you everything. Surely you deserve to hear everything, right? My head has been fucking hell. I've known I was gay and trapped with this since I was about eleven. And every single time I've thought about it I've tried to push it aside. I've tried to tell myself - nah, nah you're straight. You want pussy. You want to have sex with a girl. You fancy girls. For a while you can push it to the back of your mind and you don't think about it for a while; but then it comes back - comes back like a fucking big black cloud. This voice keeps telling you "You're gay. Just accept it - come on; you're gay." And I kept pushing it back. Saying, no, no I'm not. I'll let down my family. Let down mum, let down dad. Dad won't like it. Dad'll disown me, probably beat it out of me. Everyone'll beat it out of me. Mum'll think it's her fault. Kirsty will be ashamed of me. I'll be just like the poof up in the flats. A joke, a, a laughing stock - a side show freak. This voice is always there - reassuring you, hounding you. You try and convince yourself that maybe you just don't want sex at all. Maybe you're asexual. Right? Maybe you're just not interested in sex. Then why do I get an erection thinking about boys? Why when I'm watching porn do I look at the guys? When I watch gay porn and jack off to it - surely it's not because I'm gay? I just kind of like it sometimes. Nah, I can't be gay. Nah, then

maybe it's just a phase. But fuck - I'm eighteen and it still hasn't gone away. There's a boy in History class that I get hard when I even look at him. Hey maybe I should suck his cock.

MUM
I don't need to hear this.

BRADLEY
Yeah, you do - you'd listen to anything right? You're so selfless that you want to hear all of our shit. So this boy just happens to be gay and I actually get on quite well with him - so one day I tell him "You know - I'm gay. And I think I want you to fuck me." And I go back to his house and I suck his cock- and I fucking love it. It feels right, and he sucks my dick and I beg him 'fuck me, fuck me please.' So he fucks me. It hurts like fucking hell. Like doing a backwards poo - it literally feels like someone's ramming a brick up my arse. Eventually though - it begins to feel good and I can feel it hitting the right spot and I begin to groan and it's funny - I begin to sound like you do whenever YOU used to get fucked and scream the fucking house down. I eventually cum all over myself and then he pulls out and cums all over my face. And it's then - as I'm covered in cum and my arsehole's been fucked raw; yeah, I accept that yeah, I'm gay.

MUM has begun crying. She is almost hysterical. She is going crazy.

MUM
Why the fuck are you doing this to me? Why are you both like this? What have I done as a mother that's done this? Why are you doing this to me?!

BRADLEY
Mum - why does everything have to be about you? I've just told you something that's ruined me for years and you make it all about you -

MUM
Shut up, shut up.

KIRSTY
Are you fucking kidding me? This isn't a big deal - Bradley hasn't done anything to you.

BRADLEY
Just calm the fuck down.

MUM
You spiteful little bastard - I can't believe you'd do this to me.

BRADLEY
You know what - you're a fucking sociopath./ You're mental./ You're not right in the head./ See this is what Dad goes through day in day out, trying to keep you happy/ - trying to keep you from flying off the handle and -

MUM
Don't you fucking dare - yeah, that's it; throw what your dad says about me at me and - oh yeah, your dad goes through so much shit and pain - he hits me and abuses me me and bullies me - shut up. Shut the fuck up. SHUT THE FUCK UP!

She goes for BRADLEY. KIRSTY goes to grab MUM off of BRADLEY and MUM pushes her off. Falling back and doubling over in pain, she screams.

KIRSTY
You wonder why we both have shit?! What the fuck are we suppose to base our morals and life goals on? You? You're a selfish bitch. You only care about yourself and you make everything about you; you're a narcissist and you know what mum - we all have fucking big problems. Huge problems.

MUM
Yeah, selfish fucking cunt of a mother can't do anything right. Both my kids can't tell me anything cos mum's so selfish and wrapped up in her own shit. I CAN'T HELP IT. Maybe I'm ill - maybe I should just kill myself? Maybe I should just get a knife and slash -

KIRSTY
And here we go - we now start to enter the same phases we do with dad. You're fucking mad. Your kids are fucked up.

MUM
I'll just fucking kill myself. Then your lives will be so much fucking easier -

KIRSTY
I HAD A FUCKING ABORTION THIS AFTERNOON.

Silence. DAD has entered as she has screamed. Everyone looks at each other.

DAD
The fuck?

KIRSTY
And that was it. I had to tell them everything. About the pregnancy, about the abortion. I don't know where it came from - I just had to scream it out. I wanted to punish her, punish her for everything; all of the screaming, all of the shouting - the years of watching their phases take place. I know dad wasn't a perfect angel - but she took everything to a new level. The family and our life revolved around her. She was being abused; even though she was controlling, verbal and physical towards dad, her kids didn't care about her, even though when we tried to confide in her and open up about our lives; she made it about her. It was probably for my own fucked up head that I did it as well. I wanted to pin the blame on someone. I'd been stupid enough to get pregnant. I'd aborted the baby. But I wanted to be able to say - 'It's your fault that I've fucked up. You've fucked me up.'. To some degree it's probably true that the way we'd seen mum behave over the years had fucked us up. No child should ever grow up in a house where they regularly see their parents tearing strips out of each other. Hear them having aggressive, loud sex. See mum go so mad that dad has to physically restrain her. Get involved in the cross fire and end up with a flower pot lobbed at your fucking head. I think we'd ignored it for so long and tried to pass it off as a way of life that we'd neglected to notice that things were getting worst. In the past few months - I'd been hurt throughout one of their outbursts, it was an accident, but still; and mum had just gone crazy and attacked Bradley. This was the breaking point. Even though things were FUCKED - there was this sense of relief. We had to move forward from here.

DAD puts his hands on KIRSTY's shoulders.

DAD
I'll kill that fucking scumbag.

KIRSTY
Once dad had got over the initial/ shock.

DAD
Little/ cunt.

KIRSTY
And immense fury at Peter. He began to calm down and just held me.

DAD
You're my little girl, and even though I wouldn't have liked it - I'd have been there to hold your hand. You've been so brave; with everything. What you did that day is just another example of your courage and strength. I'm so proud of you Kirsty.

KIRSTY
Dad admitted that something needed to change and made mum go to the doctors. And now they're both on a counselling programme. Mum goes on her own and mum and dad go to one together. NHS gave us something - shock, fucking horror.

KIRSTY comes face to face with BRADLEY.

Bradley wasn't especially phased by my revelation; I think he was more happy that it took the heat off of him.

The girls enter.

JORDEN
Babe, you coming to my sixteenth?

KIRSTY
Fuck it.

CASSIE
Let's go mental.

HAYLEY
Fucking hell - go on Miley Cyrus.

KIRSTY
We sorted things with the girls. Well, sort of - I keep them at a bit of an arms length now. I don't let them influence me as much - Cassie is a much better influence on me and I'm about to sit my GCSEs...without a bump.

June 28th; I've finished all my exams. I'm getting ready to go and celebrate with Cassie. We're going for a Chinese. Mum comes into my room. She's more settled now. She's on her Quetiapine, they stabilise her moods a bit more. She's still mental sometimes, but with the counselling and the tablets - things never seem to get past phase two max.

MUM enters.

MUM
I know I've not been the best mum. I know I've let you down. I don't think I'd ever forgive...

She starts to cry.

KIRSTY
And she started to cry. I'd never seen mum cry like this. She couldn't look at me. She looked ashamed. It felt as if, just for once, I'd entered her head as a person. As her daughter. As someone she was meant to nurture. Care for. Put first. For the first time in years - I hugged her. I just hugged her. Held her tight.

The hug goes on for a moment. MUM breaks away.

MUM
But - I've just gotta know why.

KIRSTY
Why what?

MUM
You know your aunty Jessica?

KIRSTY
Yeah?

MUM
She couldn't have kids. Her and Vince were desperate for kids for years. They kept trying and trying. She spent years not feeling like a woman. Feeling like she'd failed - thinking that she'd let Vince down. The heartache and hurt almost destroyed their marriage. They ended up adopting.

KIRSTY
What? Charlie is?

MUM
Had it not been for someone giving away their child; giving the gift of a child - then they would never have got the one thing they both desperately wanted. They'd have never been parents. I just don't understand how you could get rid of that baby. Think of how many people need a child - you could have given a gift to someone else.

KIRSTY
Yeah, yeah maybe I could have.

Mum - do you regret having us?

MUM
What? I - never. I know I'm crazy. I know I've put us through a lot, but I never regret having you two. I could never live without you two.

KIRSTY

That's why I did it Mum. The minute I found out I was pregnant. I knew - it was my baby. A baby that I was gonna have to carry for nine months. Have inside me. Have need me. I'd have walked around as a circus show attraction. "Hey look, it's that girl - pregnant at sixteen." I'd be judged, shamed, berated for the best part of a year. It would affect me getting into college or sixth form. I wouldn't be able to get a job once the baby was born. How could I provide for the baby? Could I have brought it into our house? Would that be fair? All that worry - for a child to grow up in the same place I did. The same background, the same shit. Growing up with nan and grandad trying to kill each other. Knowing that I'll have to ponce and scrounge to give this baby any kind of life. And yet, somehow - once that baby was handed to me. I know, that I could never hand it over. Handing it over would be like giving my heart. The doctor might as well slam his hands into my chest and pull it out. Rip it through the muscle and the fat. Pull it out the ribcage, and whilst he's at it - pierce it into the rib cage. And I know, I know it's selfish. Yeah - that baby may not have had to have the same life as me; because it would probably go to parents who didn't have to scrimp and save - they'd probably be able to give the baby everything it ever needed. But I couldn't do that to myself. I couldn't go through that pain; because what would I have left once I handed that baby over? After not getting into college, or getting a job because of being pregnant. The baby would be gone - with my pierced and broken heart and I'd be trapped here. That baby had two choices; be aborted or grow up on the estate with us. There was no chance I could have given that baby away.

We're all trapped here. It's just the way it goes round here. You had us. You stayed here on the estate. Bradley fought for years to come to terms with his sexuality cos he knows he'll be a target for abuse - it ain't like that everywhere Mum. Look at all the other girls round this area. Pregnant, and what they gonna do? How are they gonna get out of this? There ain't no escape. Council mums with fags hanging out there mouths. People living off the dole. Drinking down the shipyard every night because there ain't nothing else to look forward to. Scared to get a job cos you're gonna lose your benefits, yet when you work you won't earn as much as your benefits - so you're always trapped on the dole if you wanna live. I ain't choosing the easy option. I wanna get out of here - I don't wanna be trapped. Every one else may have settled for this life. But I'm not gonna. I'm getting out and I'm claiming something that ain't benefits. I'm claiming a life for myself; the others may be happy to stay here and drown in this sea of grey and poverty. But I won't. I want a better life.

Blackout.

www.ingramcontent.com/pod-product-compliance
Lightning Source LLC
Chambersburg PA
CBHW071458080526
44587CB00014B/2146